I0476185

SkullDoodles

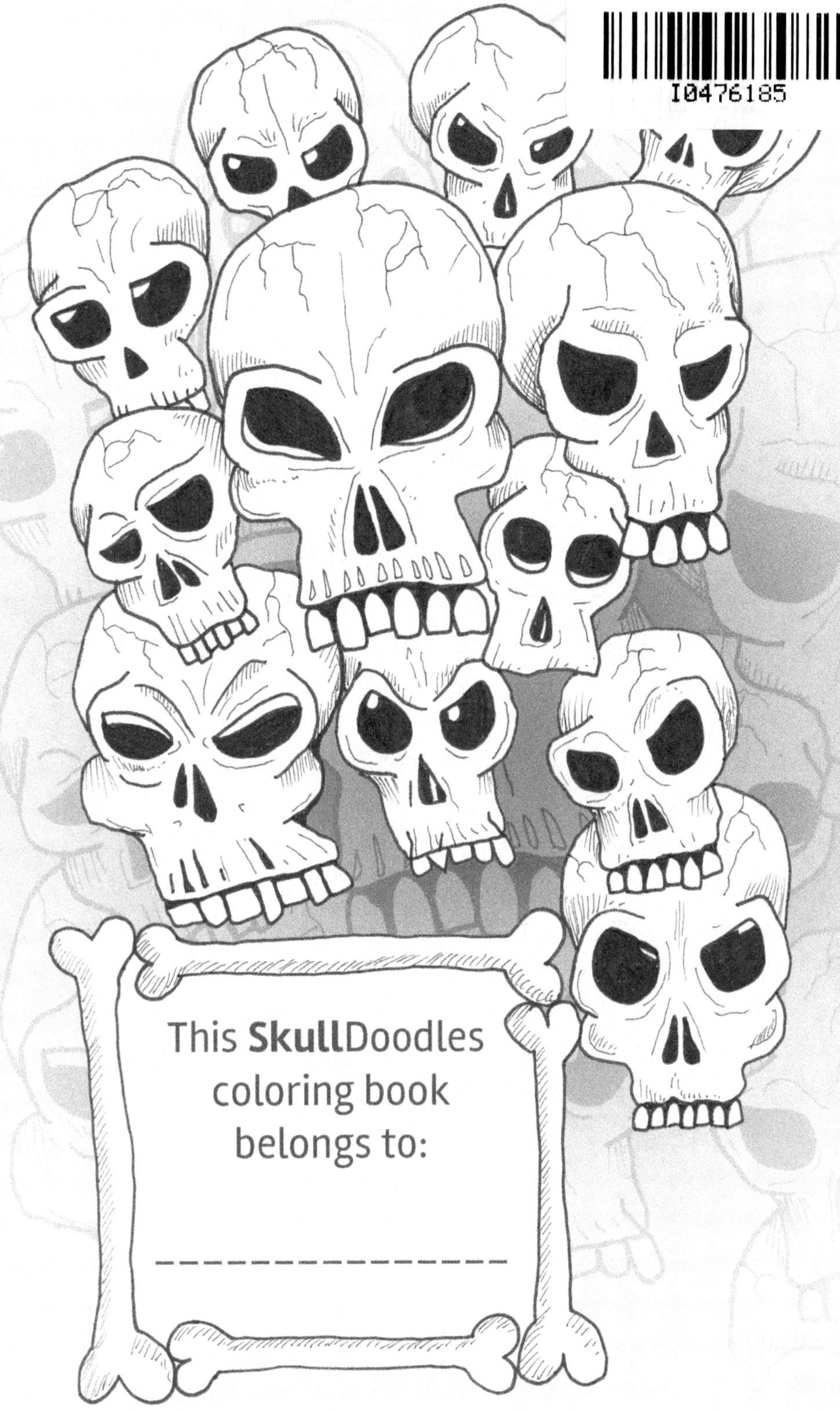

This **Skull**Doodles
coloring book
belongs to:

_____

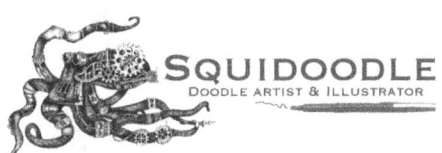

SQUIDOODLE
DOODLE ARTIST & ILLUSTRATOR

SkullDoodles
Squidoodle's Book of Skulls

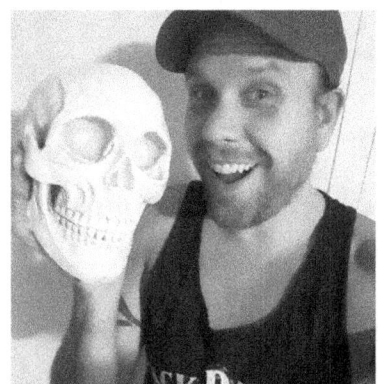

Yo! Thanks for buying Skulldoodles!

If you've ever owned one of my books before you'll know that **everything** is hand-drawn by me. I **never** use clipart, stock images or the work of other artists.

In this book you'll find over thirty unique illustrations for coloring in; from skull mandalas, skull tattoos, dinosaur skulls, graffiti designs, mechanical skulls, flowery skulls and so much more.

I've always loved skulls. Not in a particularly morbid way, but skull tattoos and sugar skulls are pretty awesome looking. When I planned to do a skull coloring book I faced one major problem: You guessed it... skulls are meant to be white! So I quickly realised the book would have to incorporate lots of different ideas and backgrounds for coloring. I didn't want to just create a book of sugar skulls, so I've tried to include not only human skulls but a unicorn skull and a dinosaur skull as well! I've also made sure to include some flowery backgrounds to color as well as patterned backgrounds.

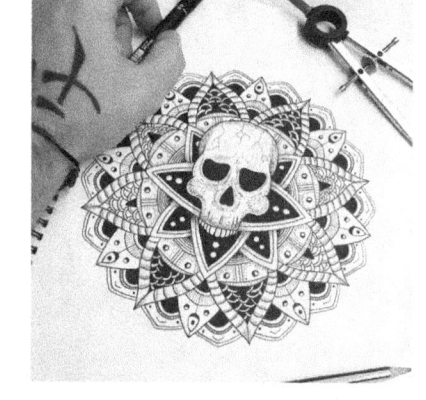

There are a couple of people I want to thank first in helping with this book. I started asking around the coloring groups on facebook for ideas for my next book and a guy by the name of **Sean Barthel** originally came up with the Skulls book idea, so, Sean, thanks buddy. The front cover for this book features the excellent coloring skills of **Nicola Tagger** who, I think you'll agree, has done an amazing job.

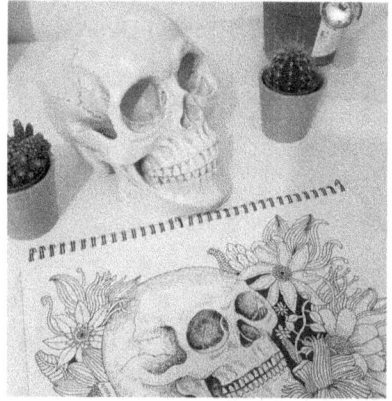

As with my previous books, there are two people who always get thanked. These two people are the first to see my illustrations. They give me ideas, tell me when they think things need changing, and they are always the first two people to get copies of a new book. They color them brilliantly, they copy the drawings themselves, and they seem to think their old dad is a famous artist. So to my beautiful daughters **Poppy and Lola,** I'll keep making books as long as you two keep coloring them.

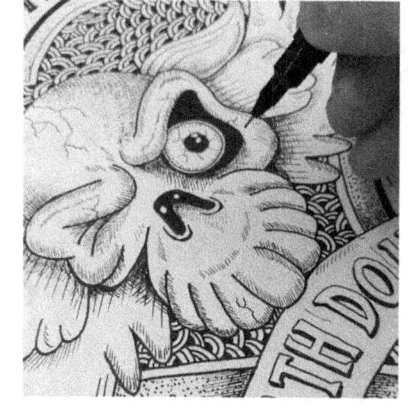

Squidoodle
xxx

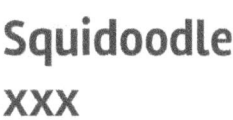

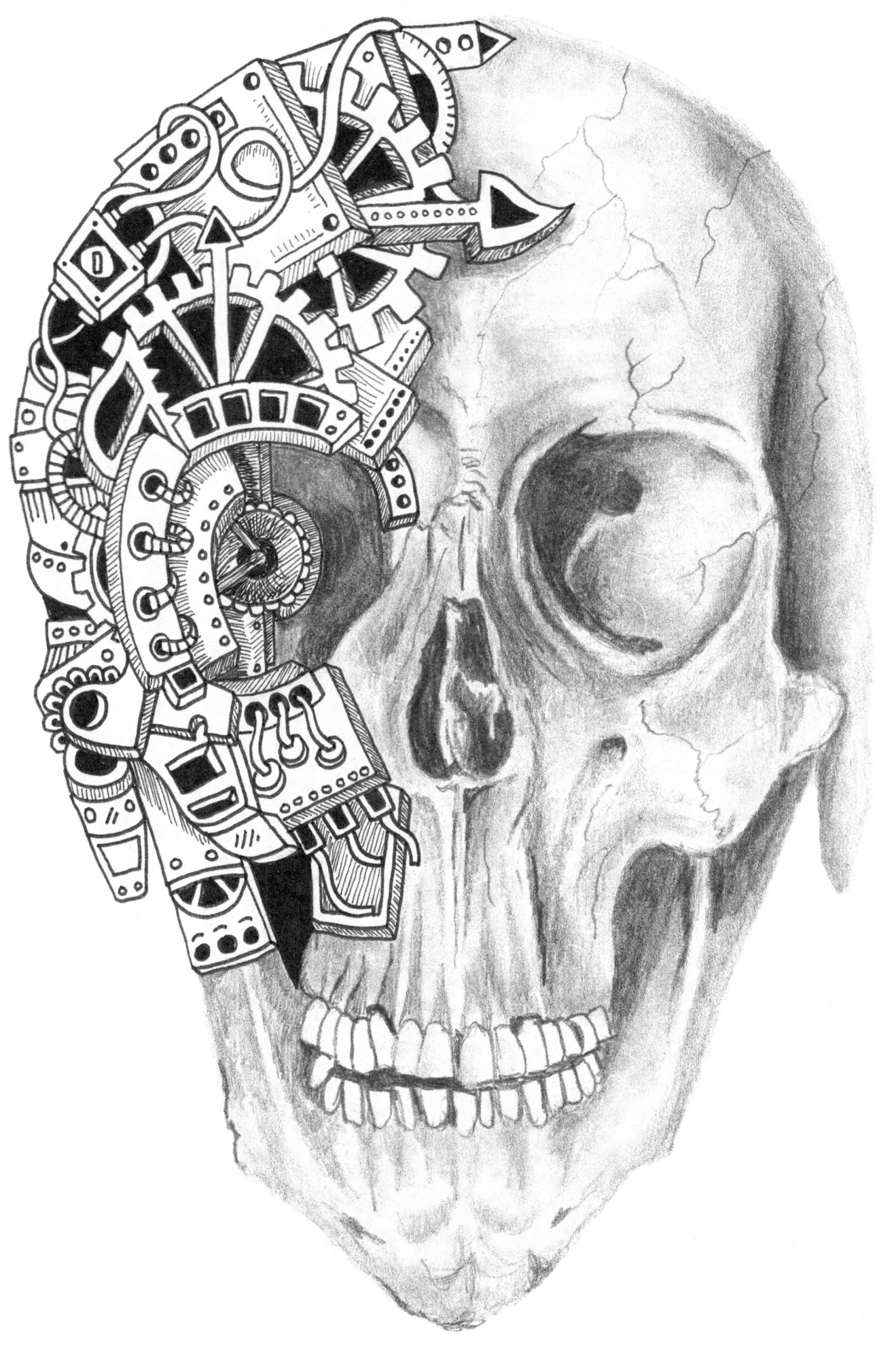

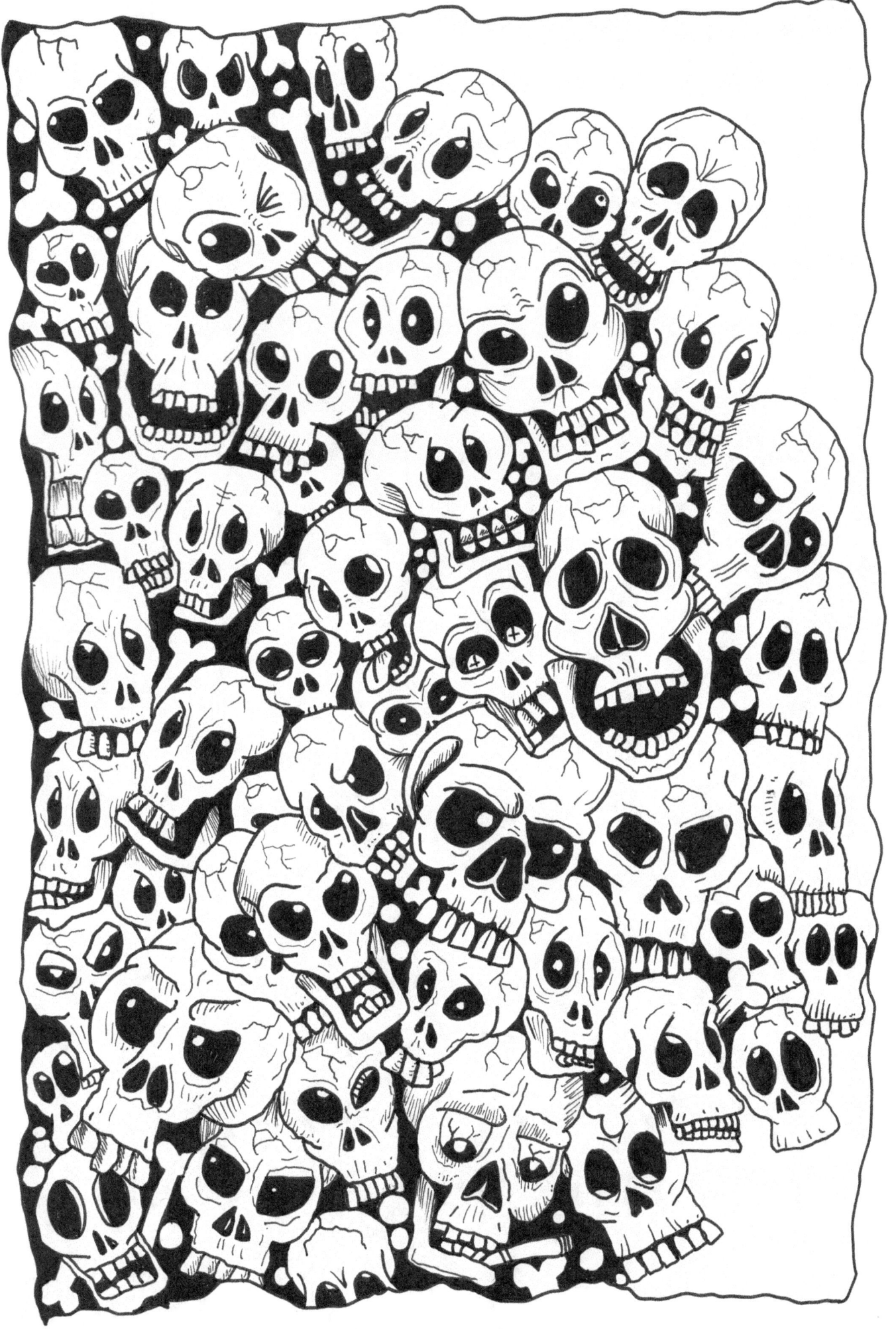

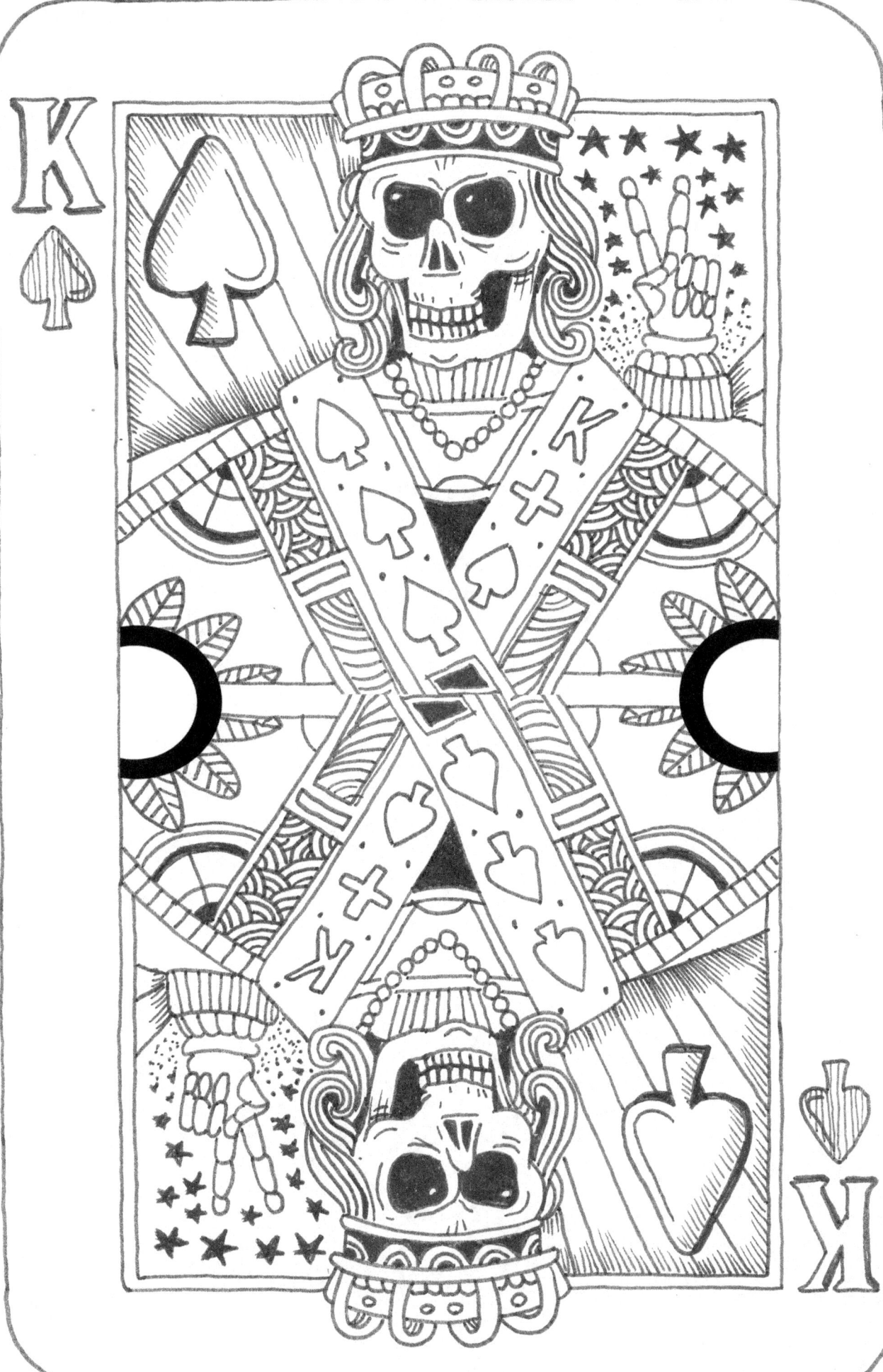

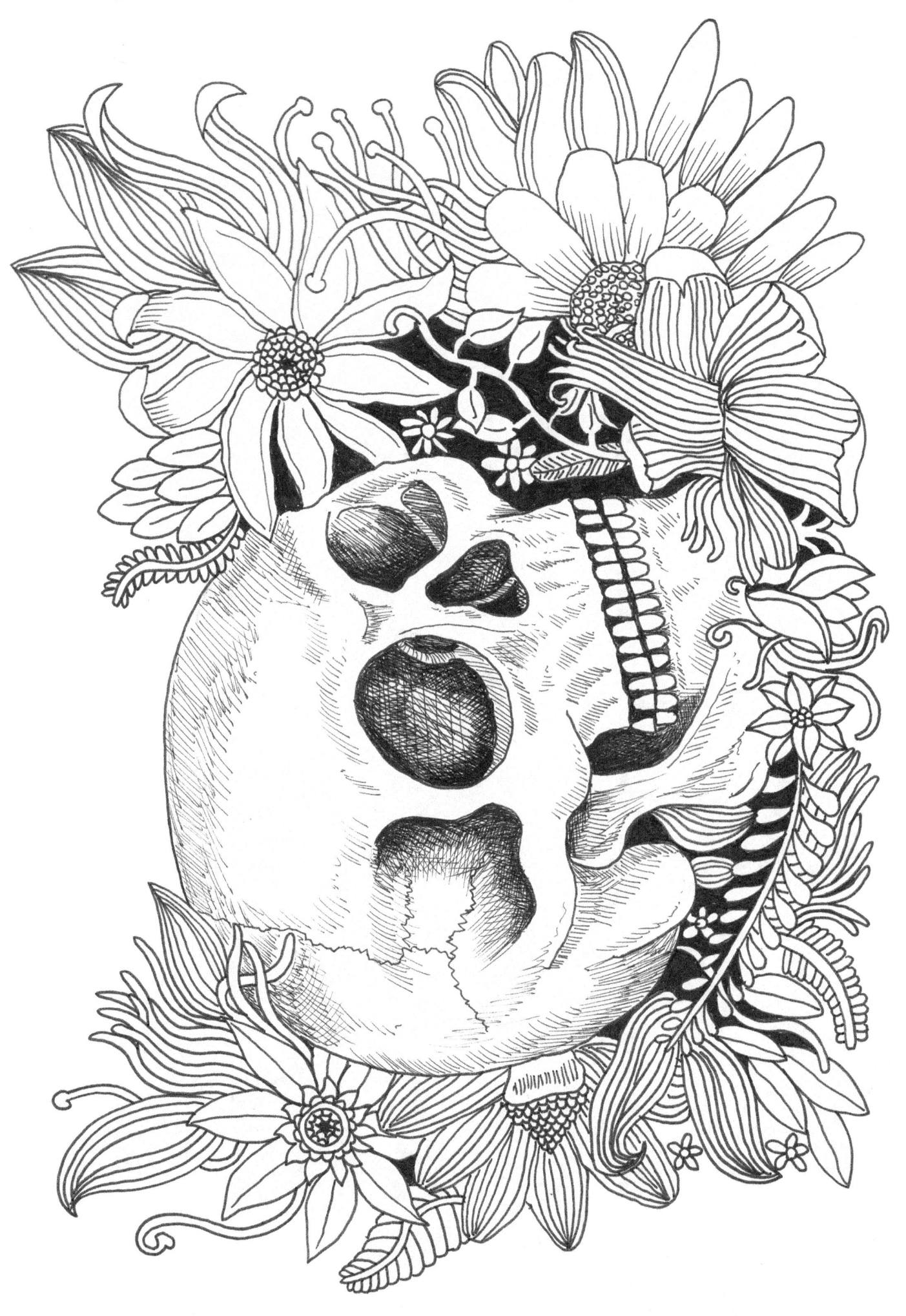

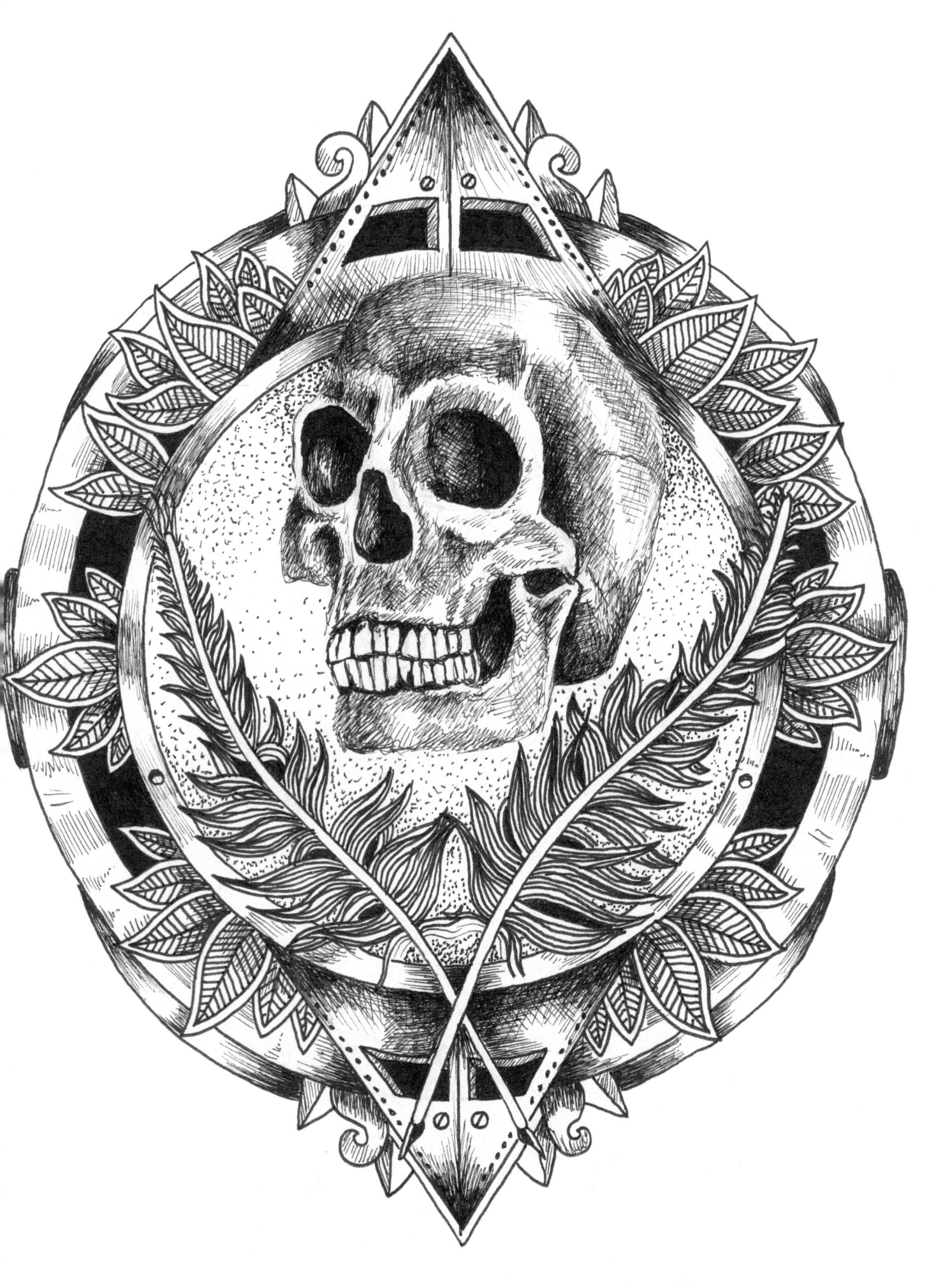

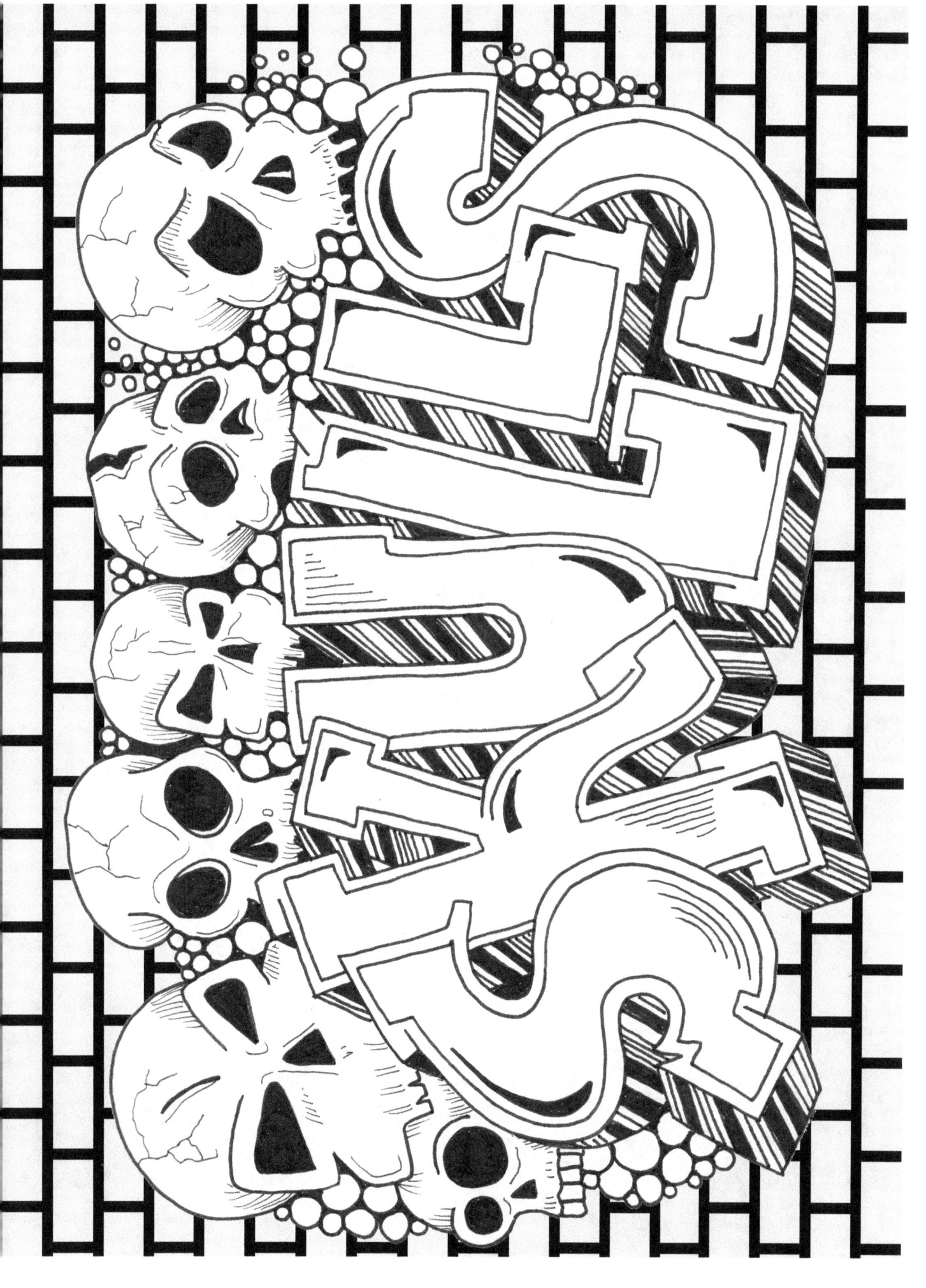

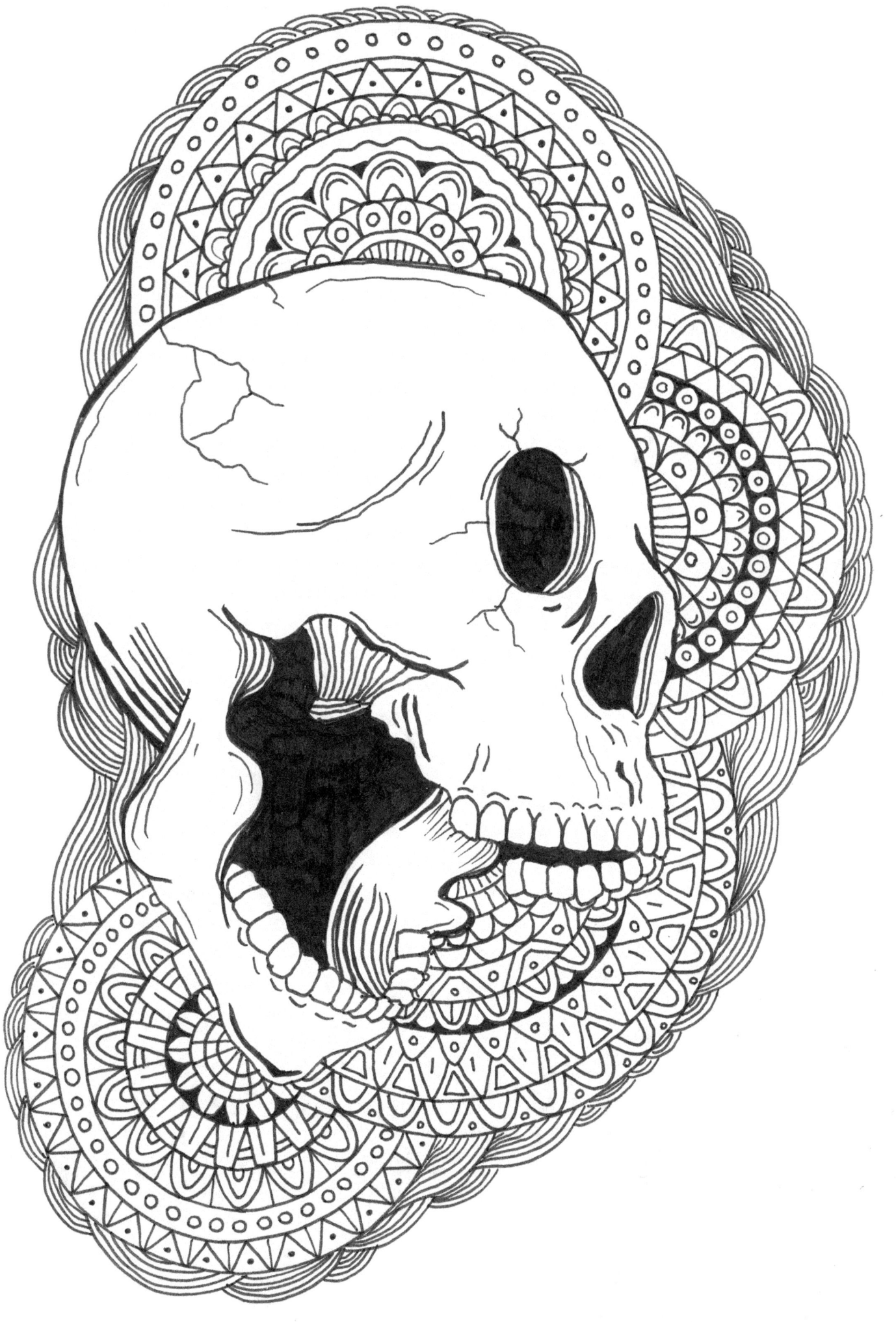

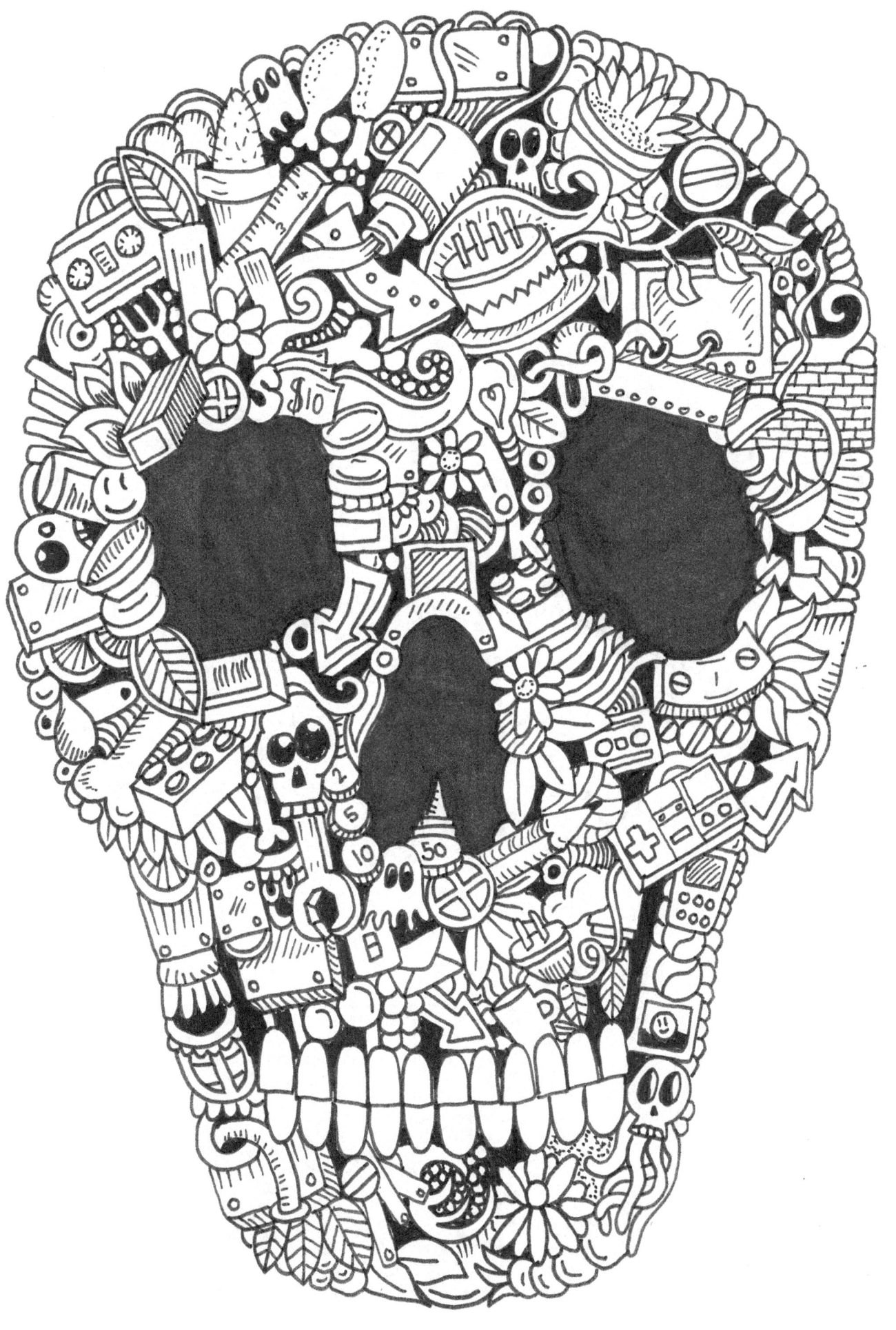

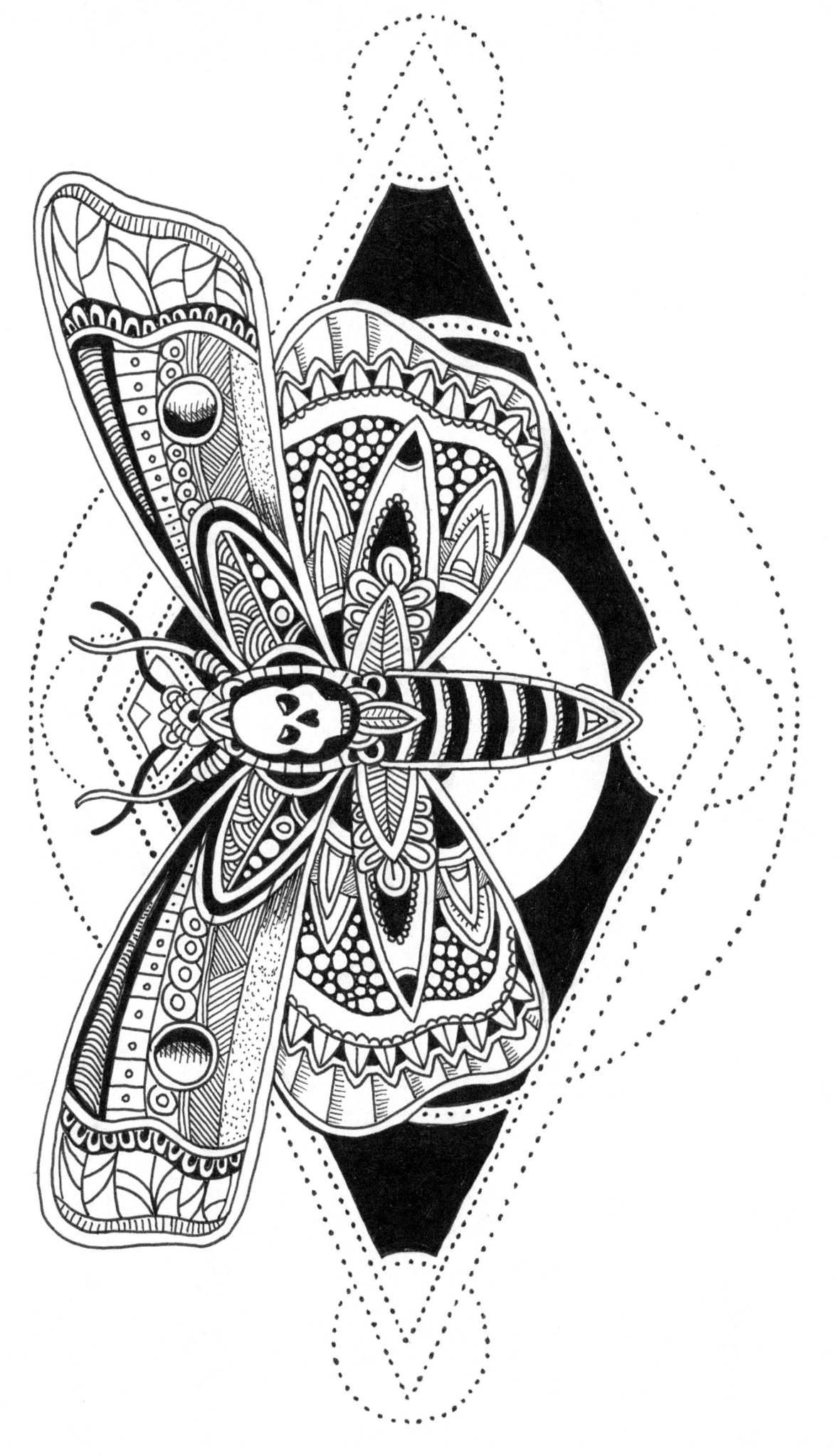

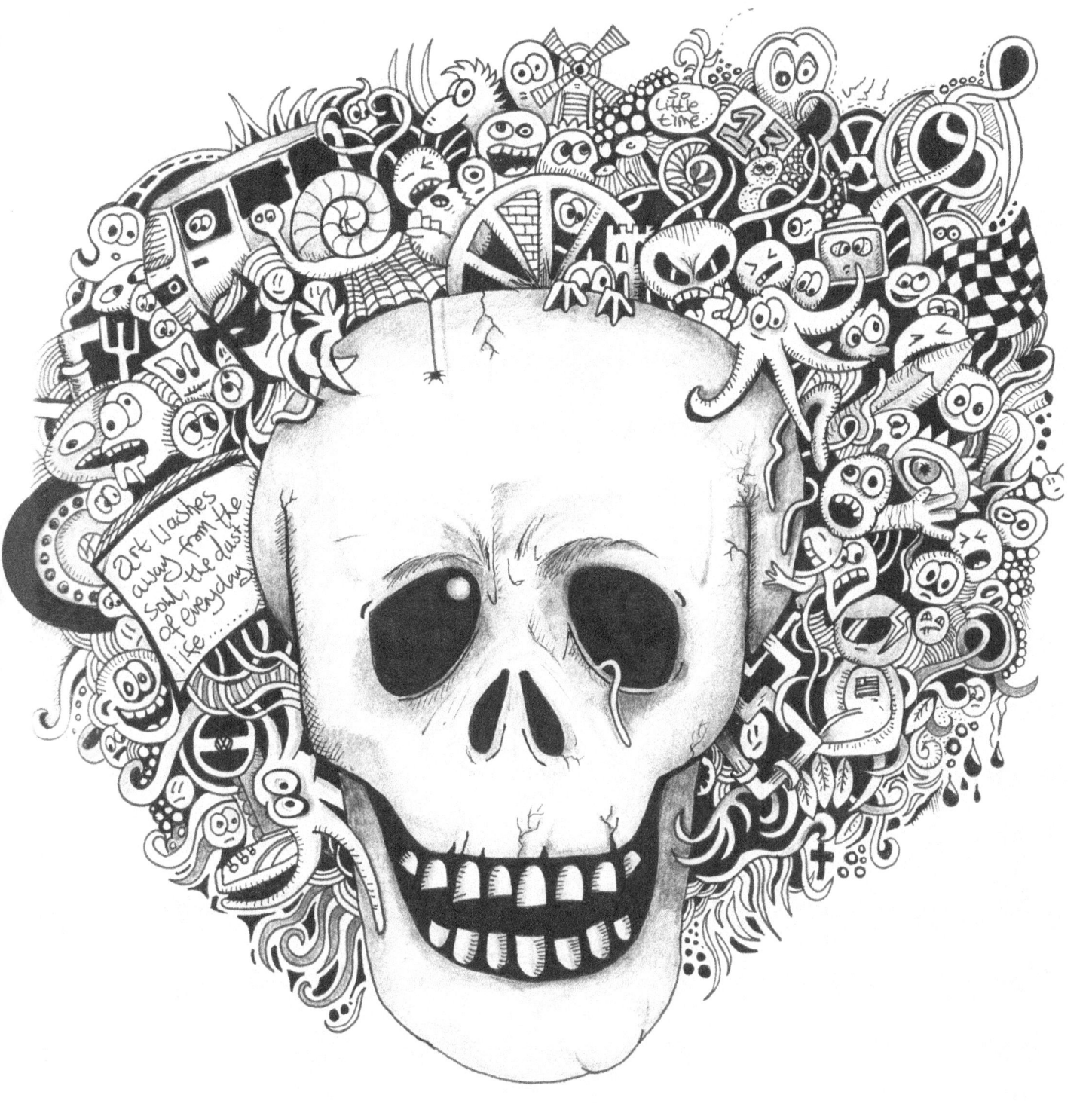

I have a lot
on my mind.

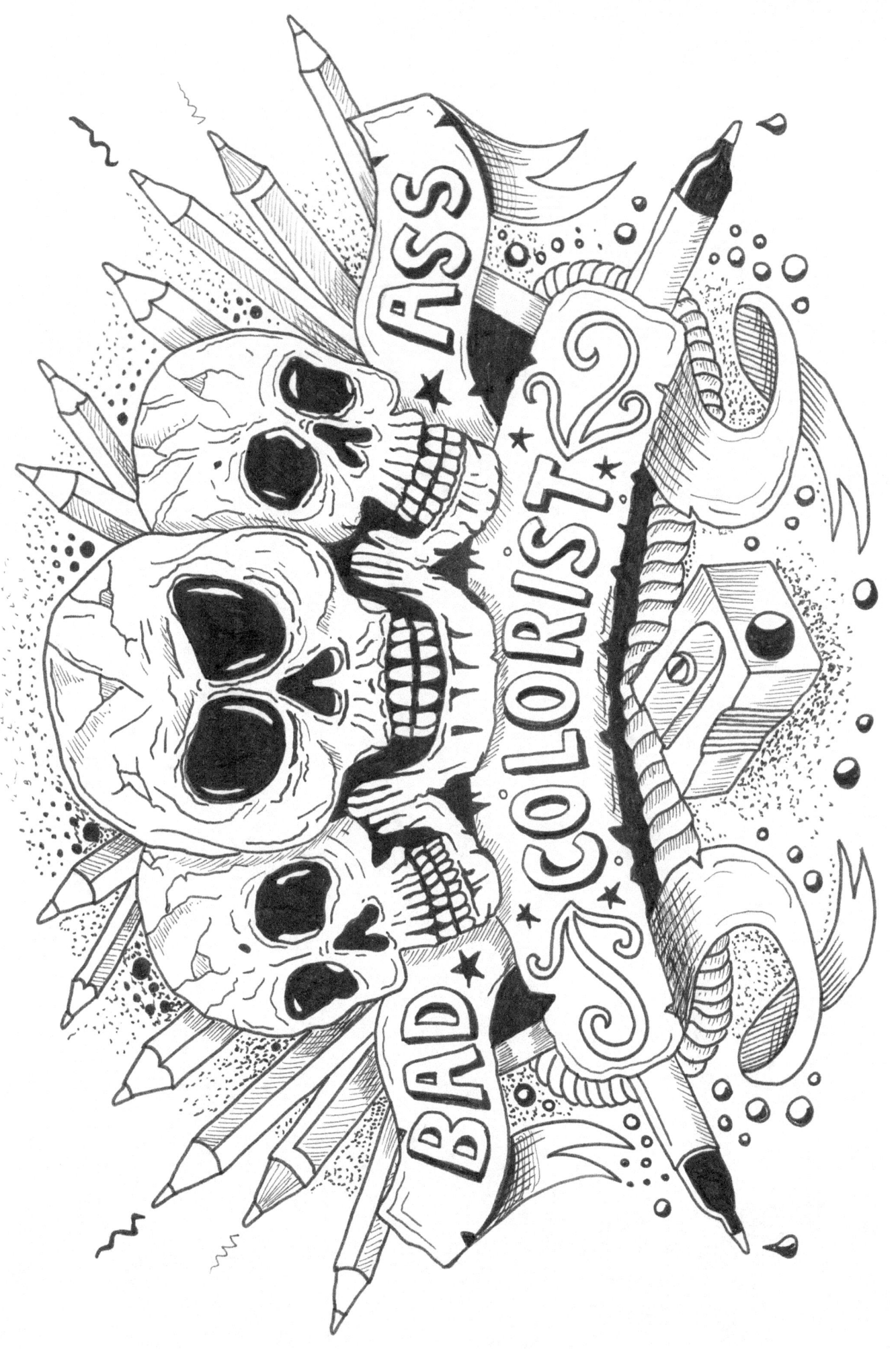

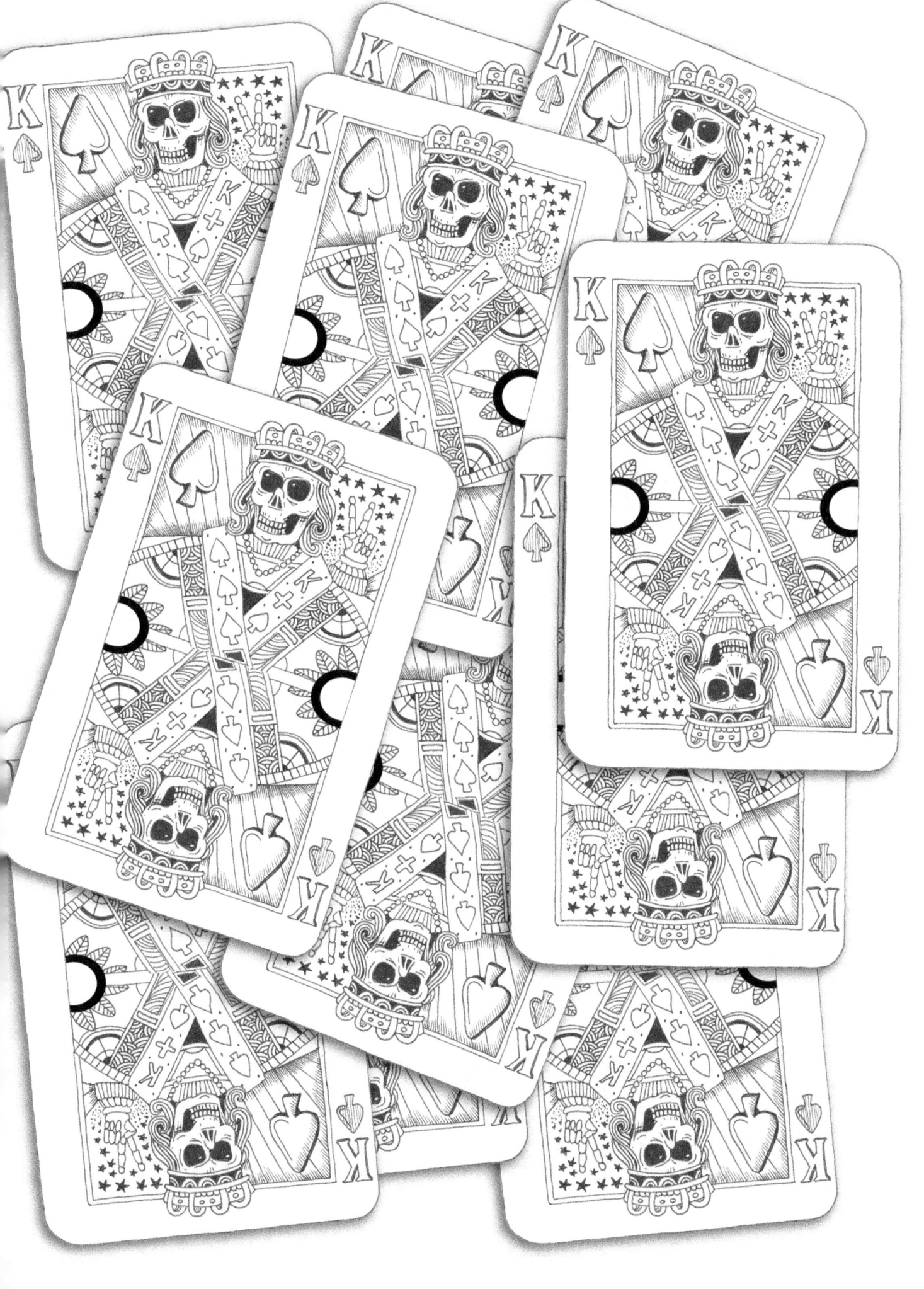

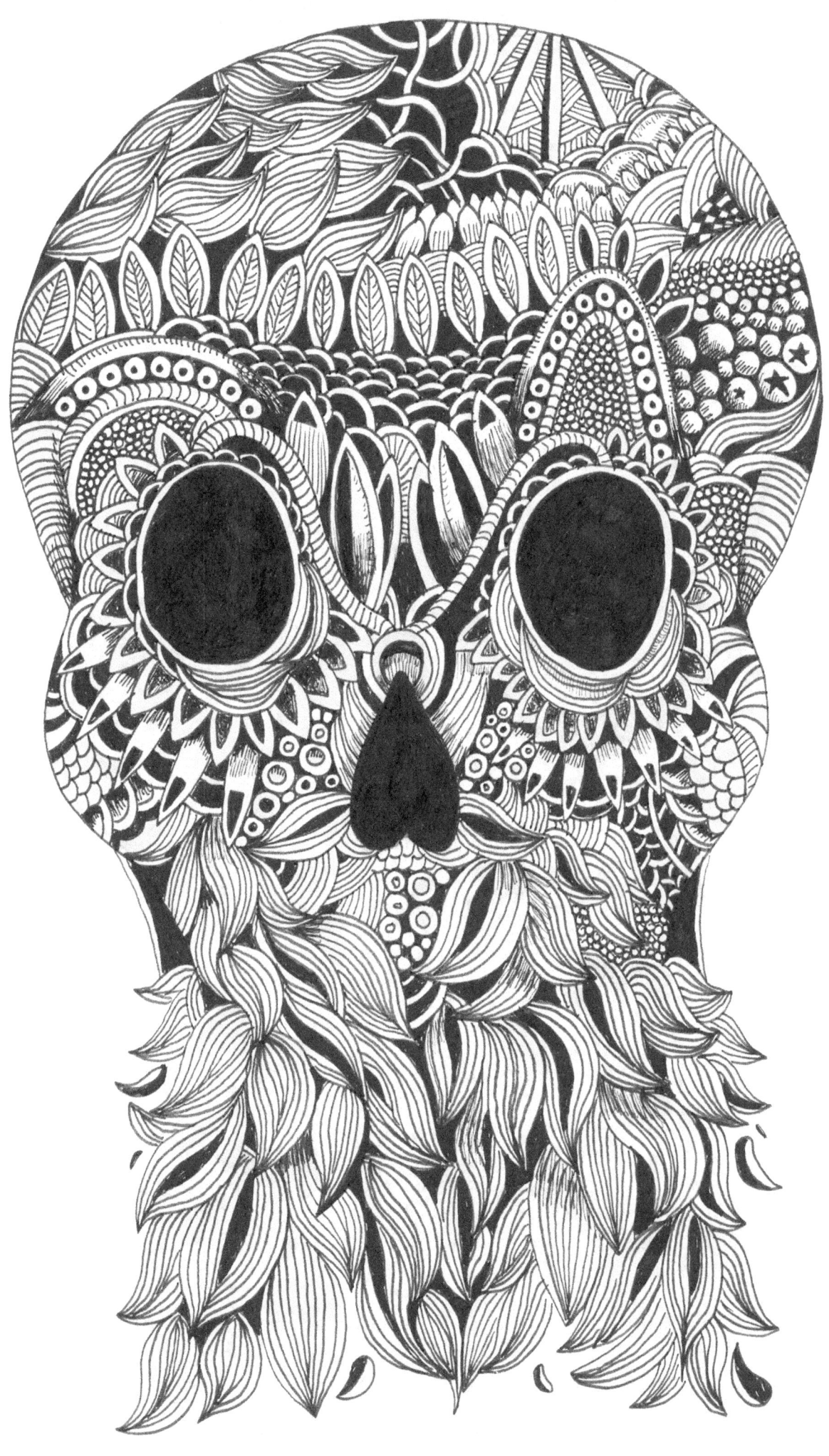

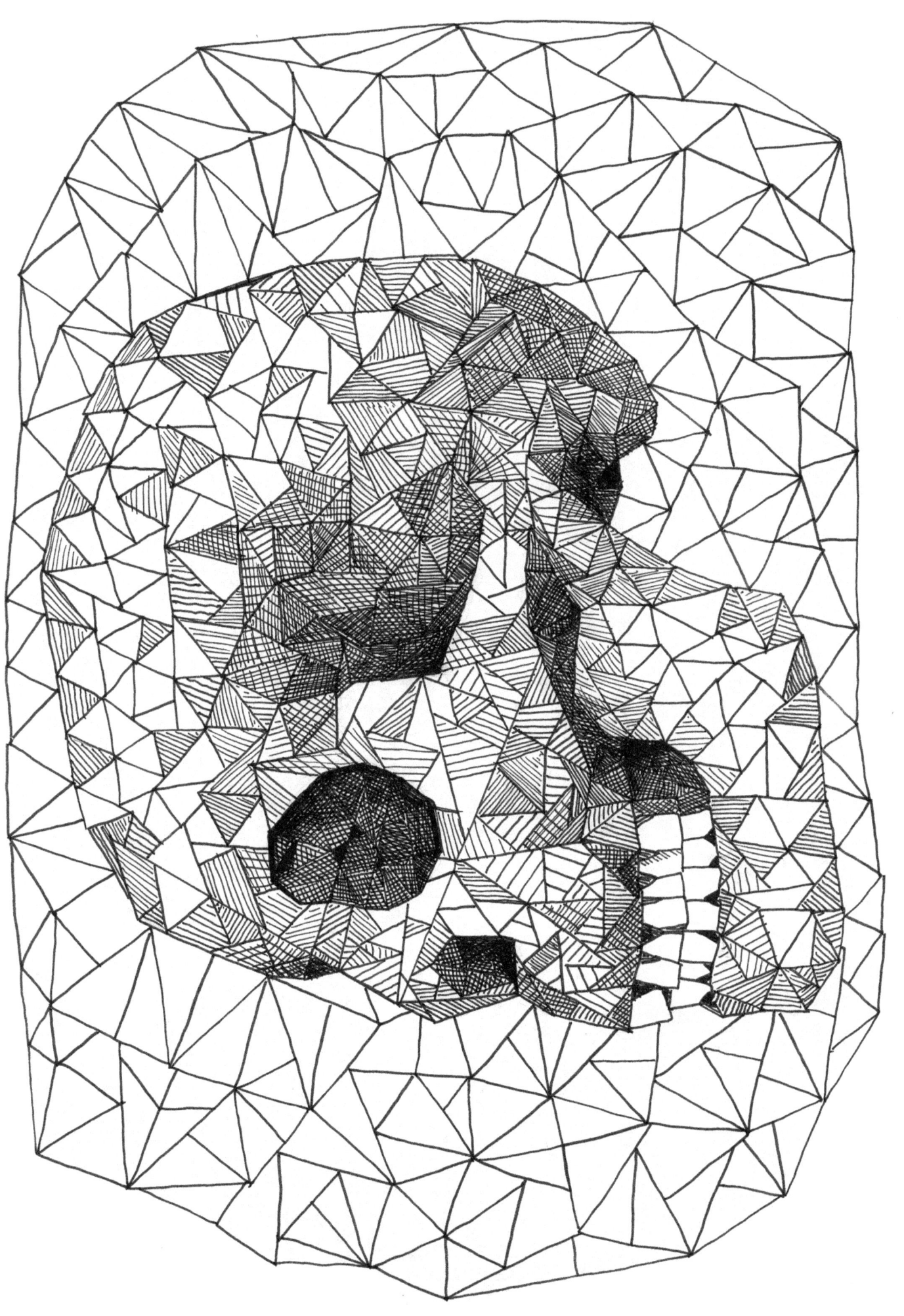

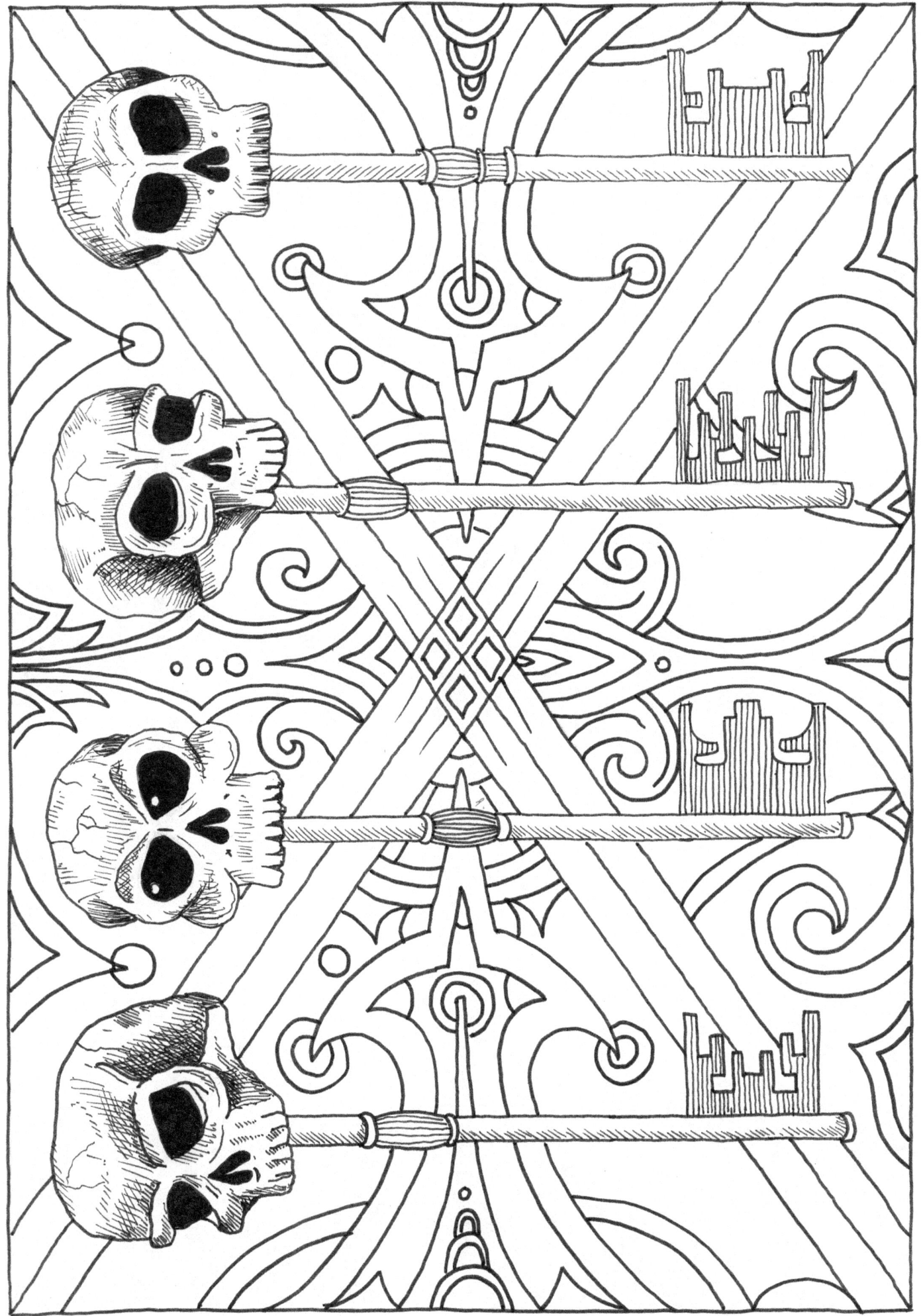

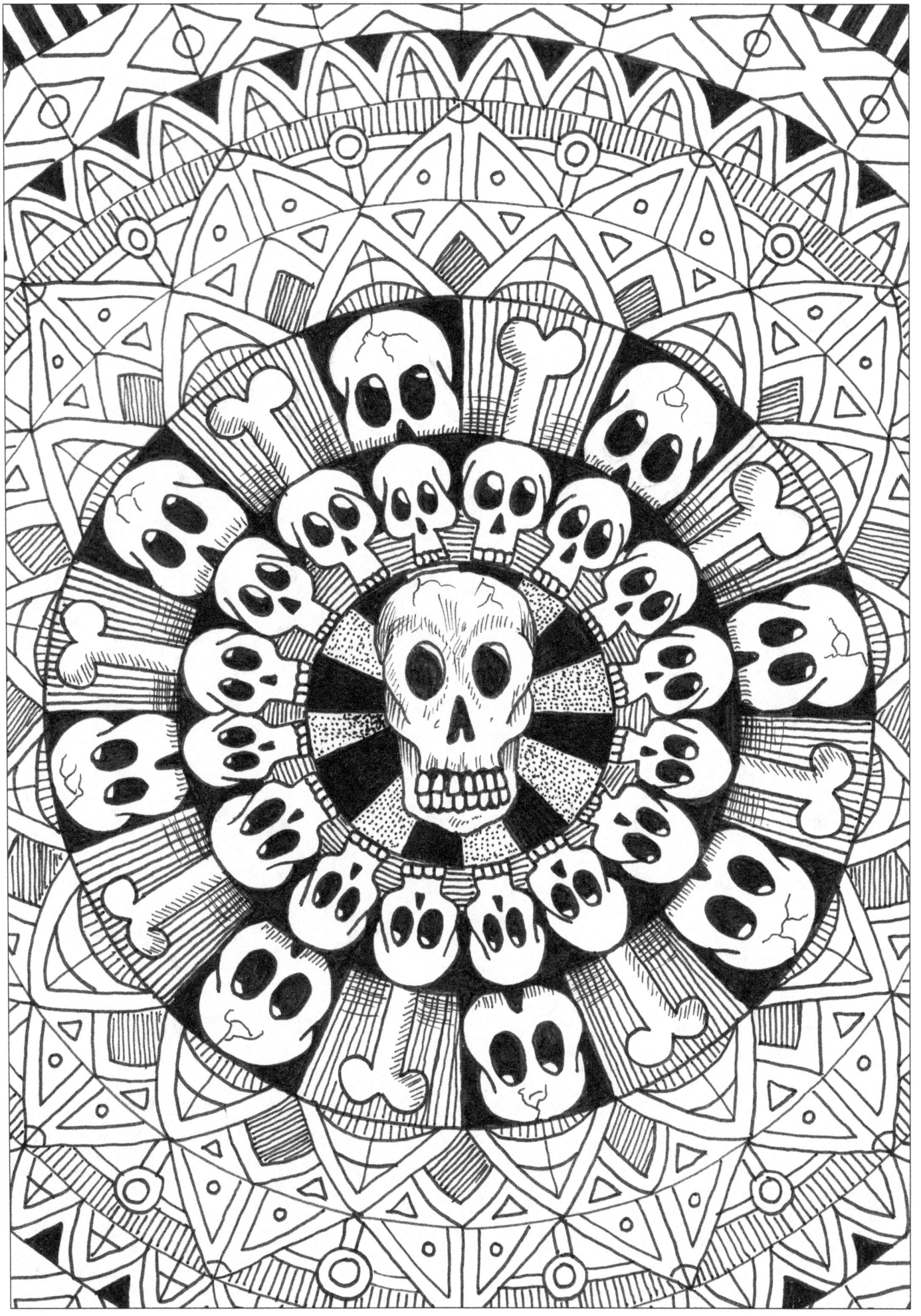

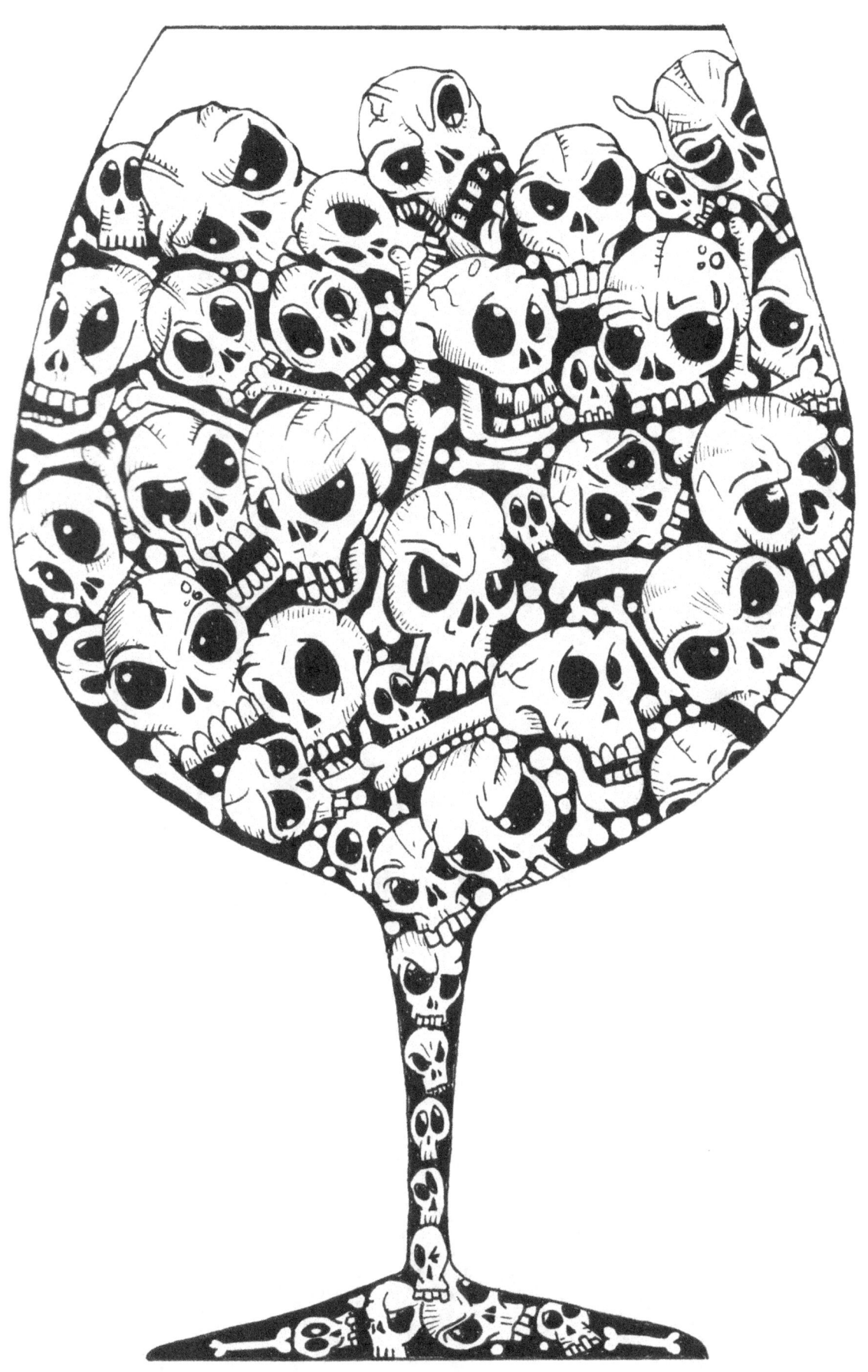

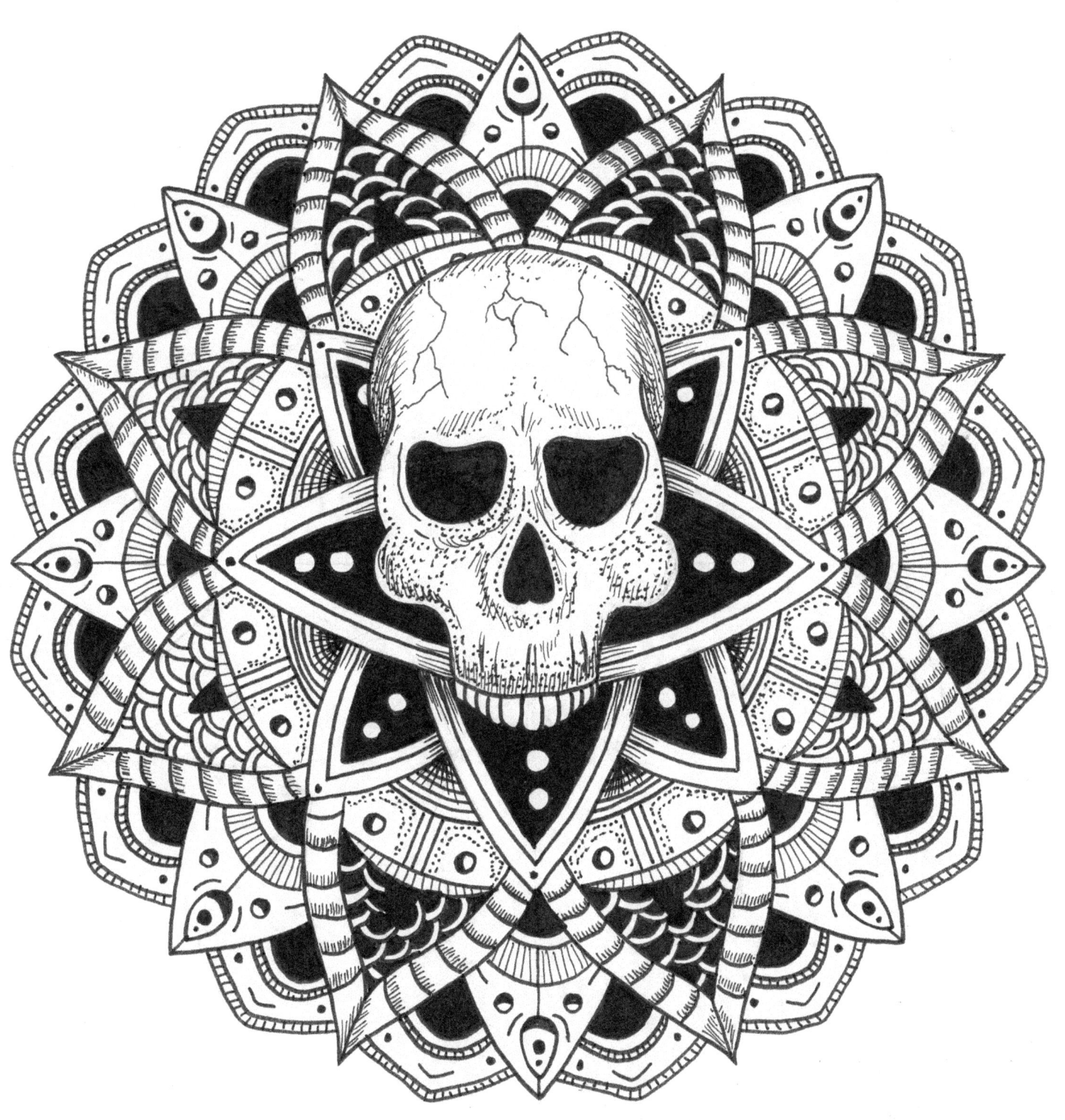

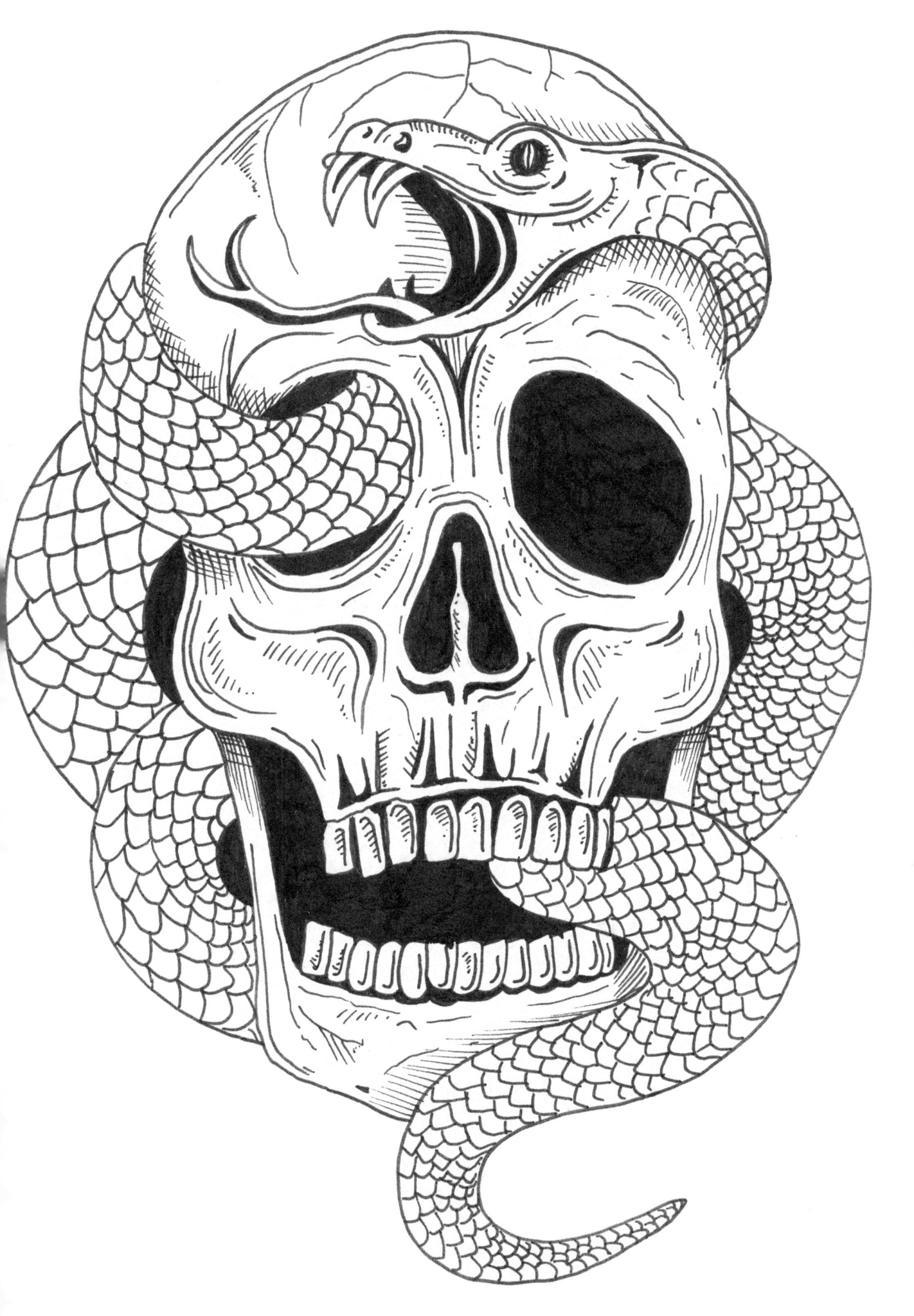

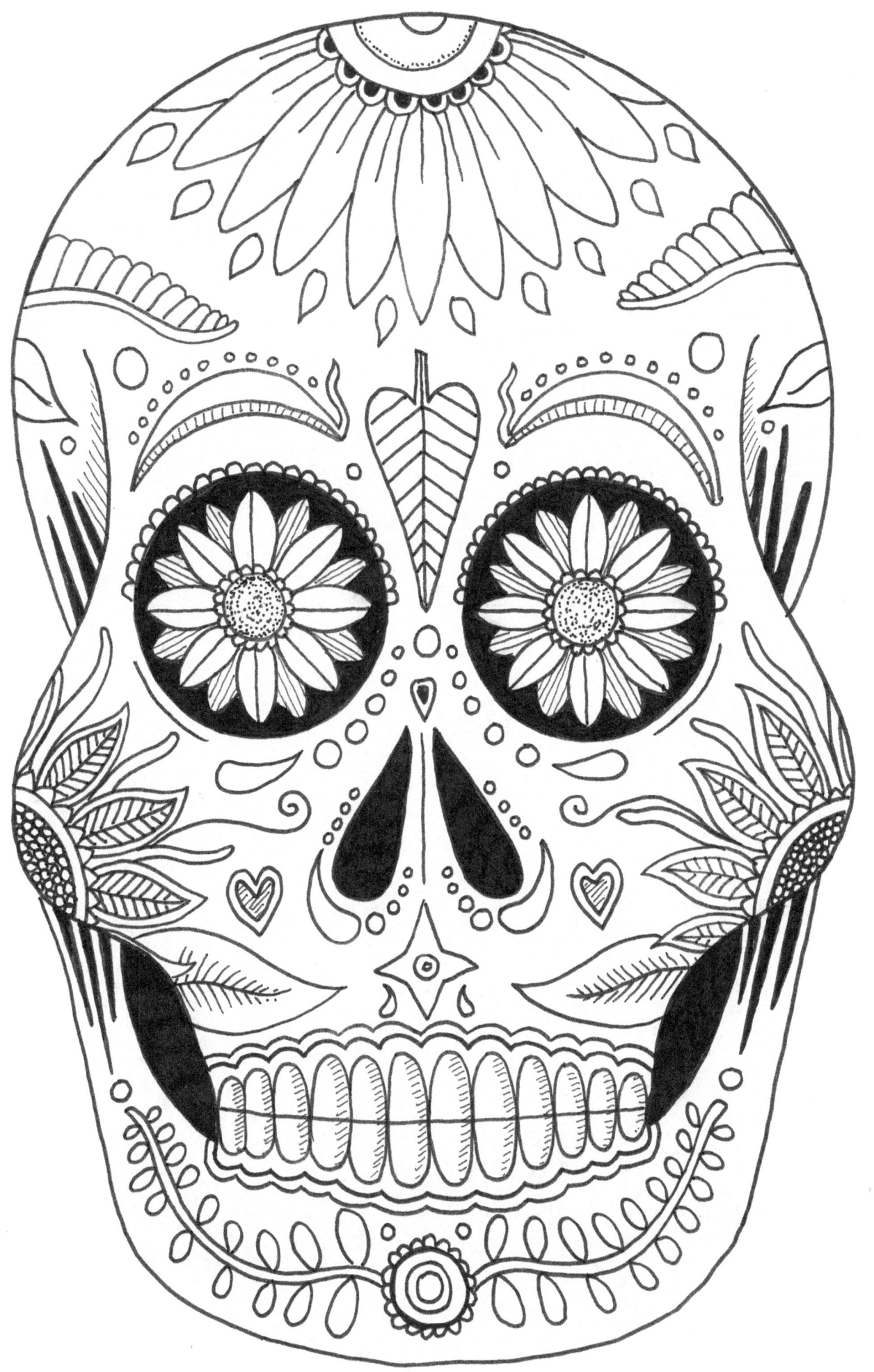

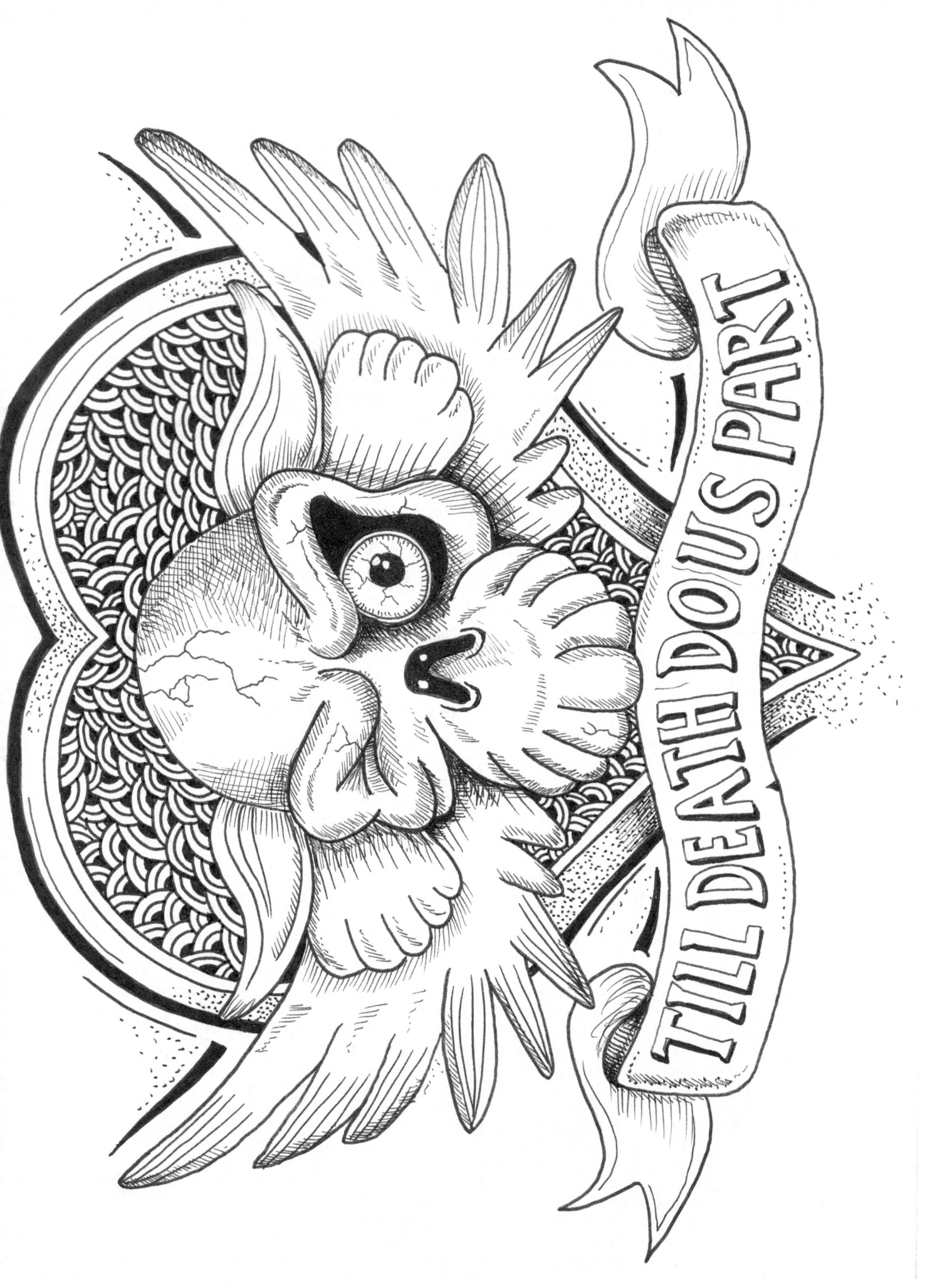

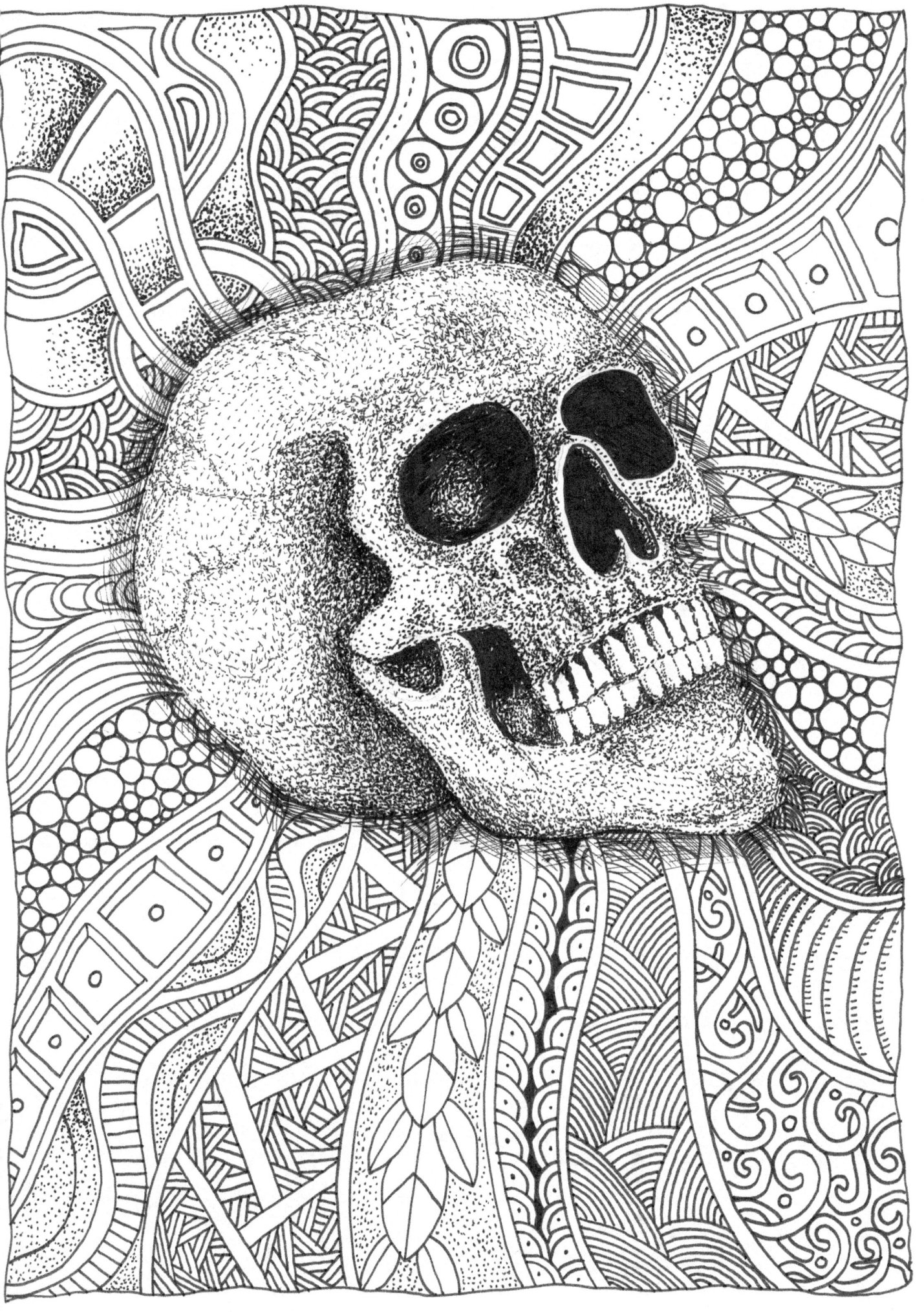

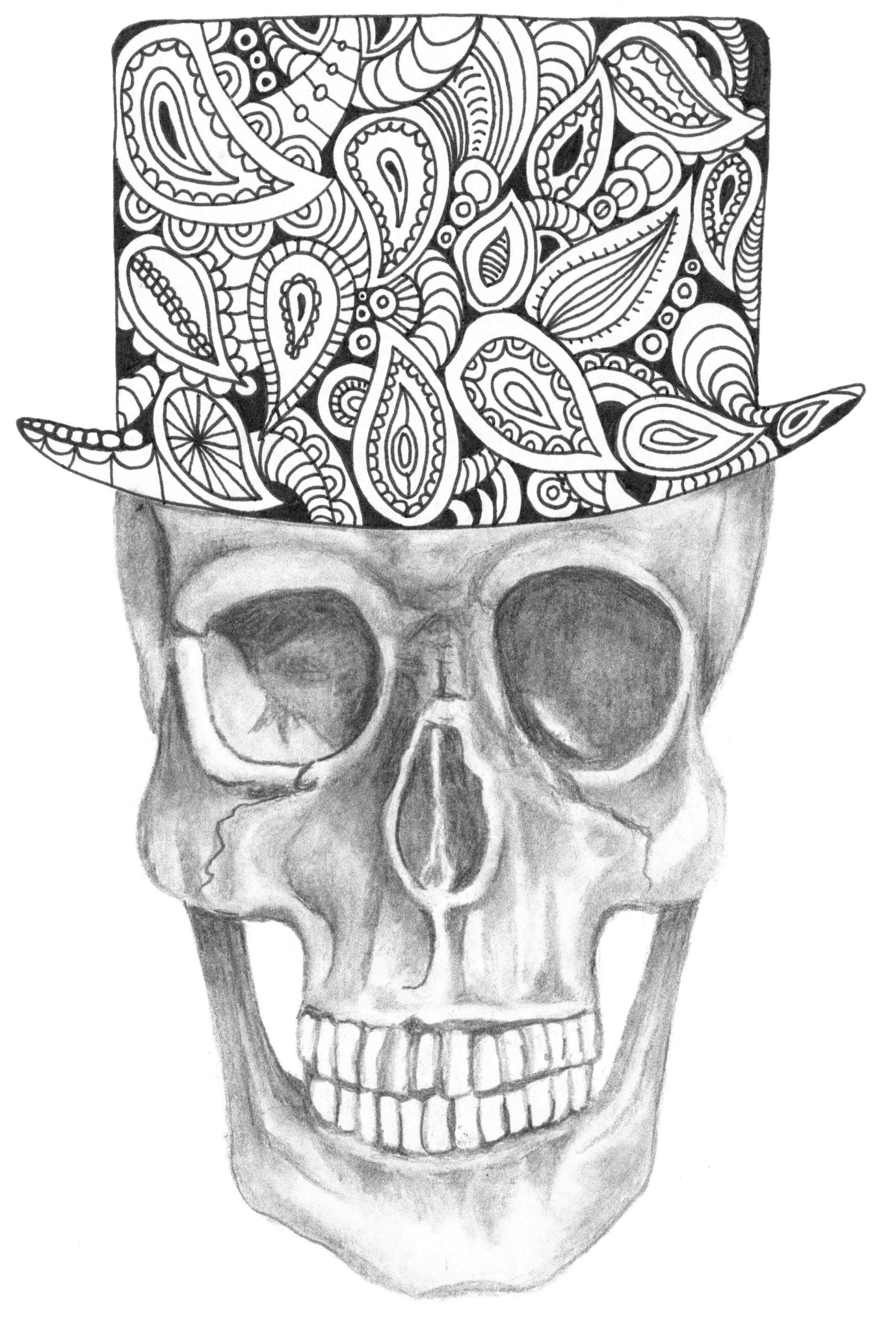

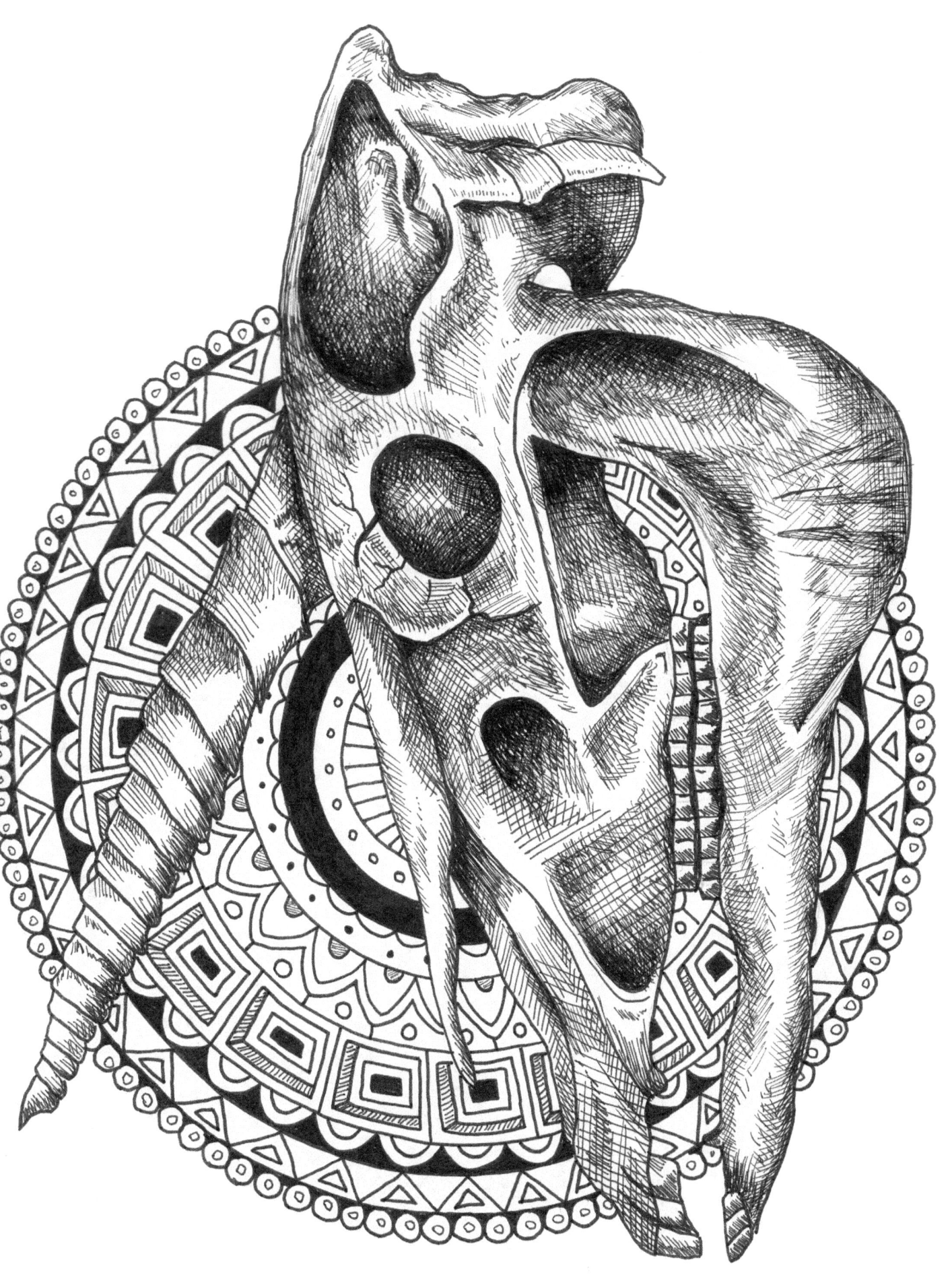

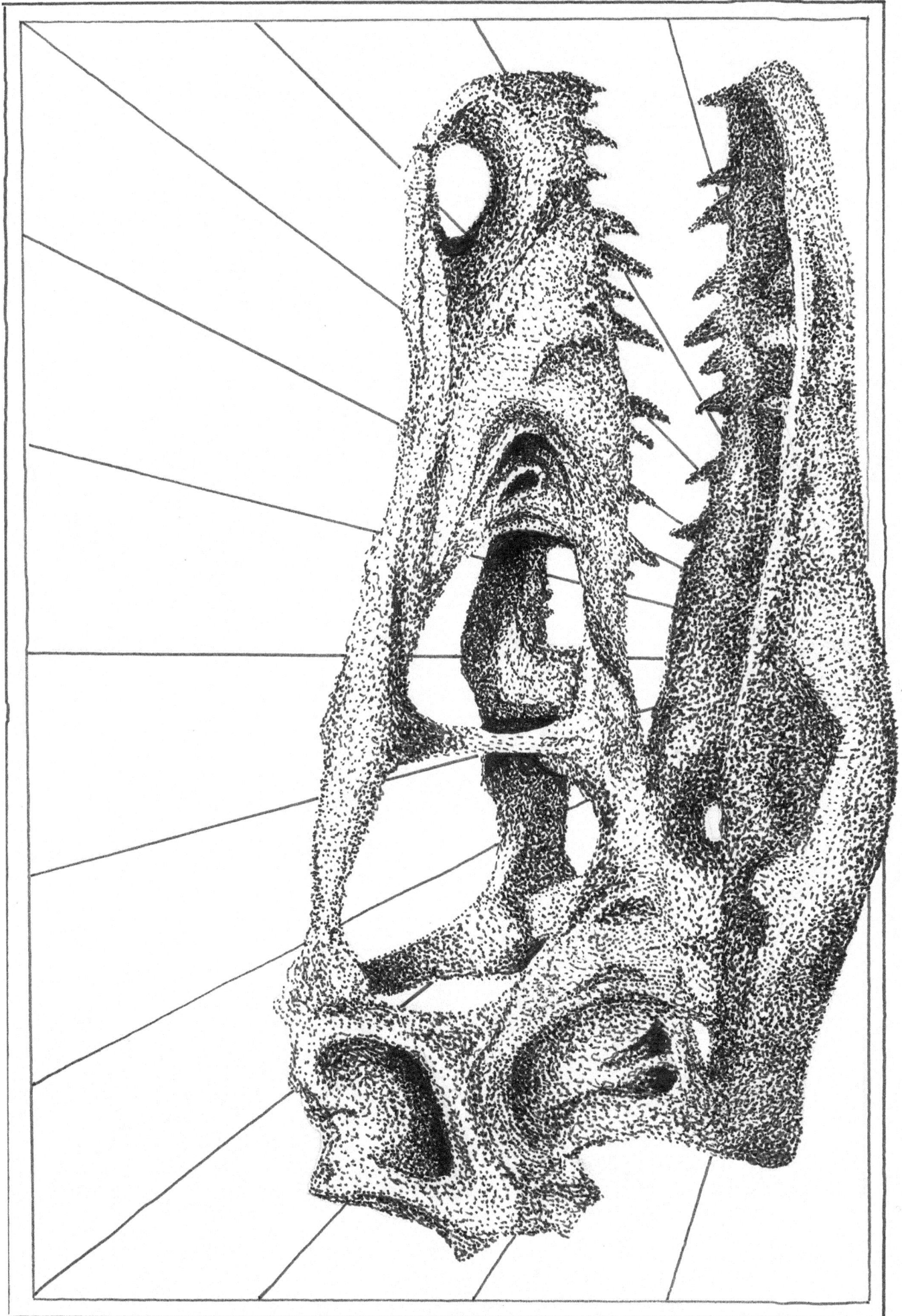

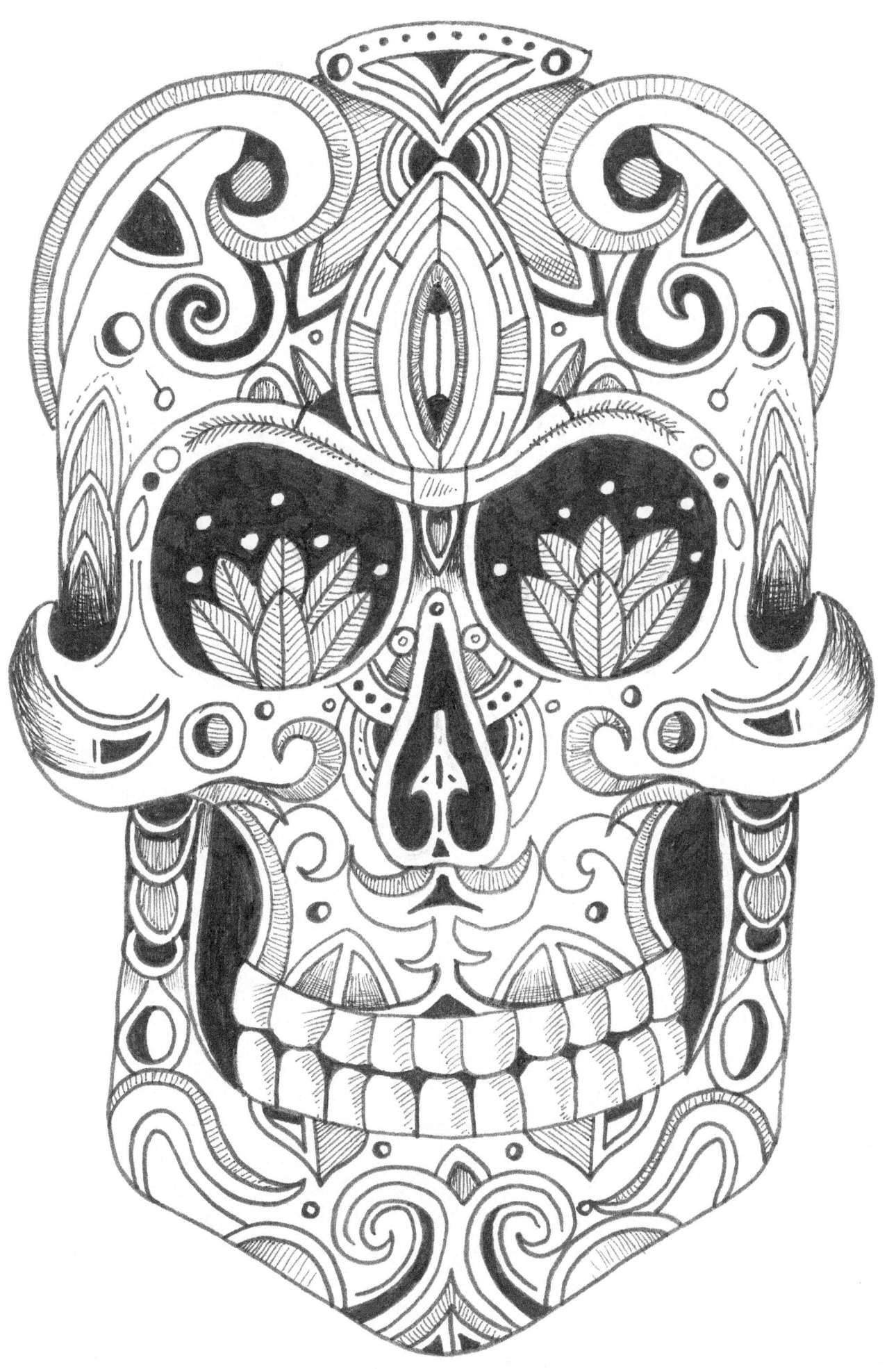

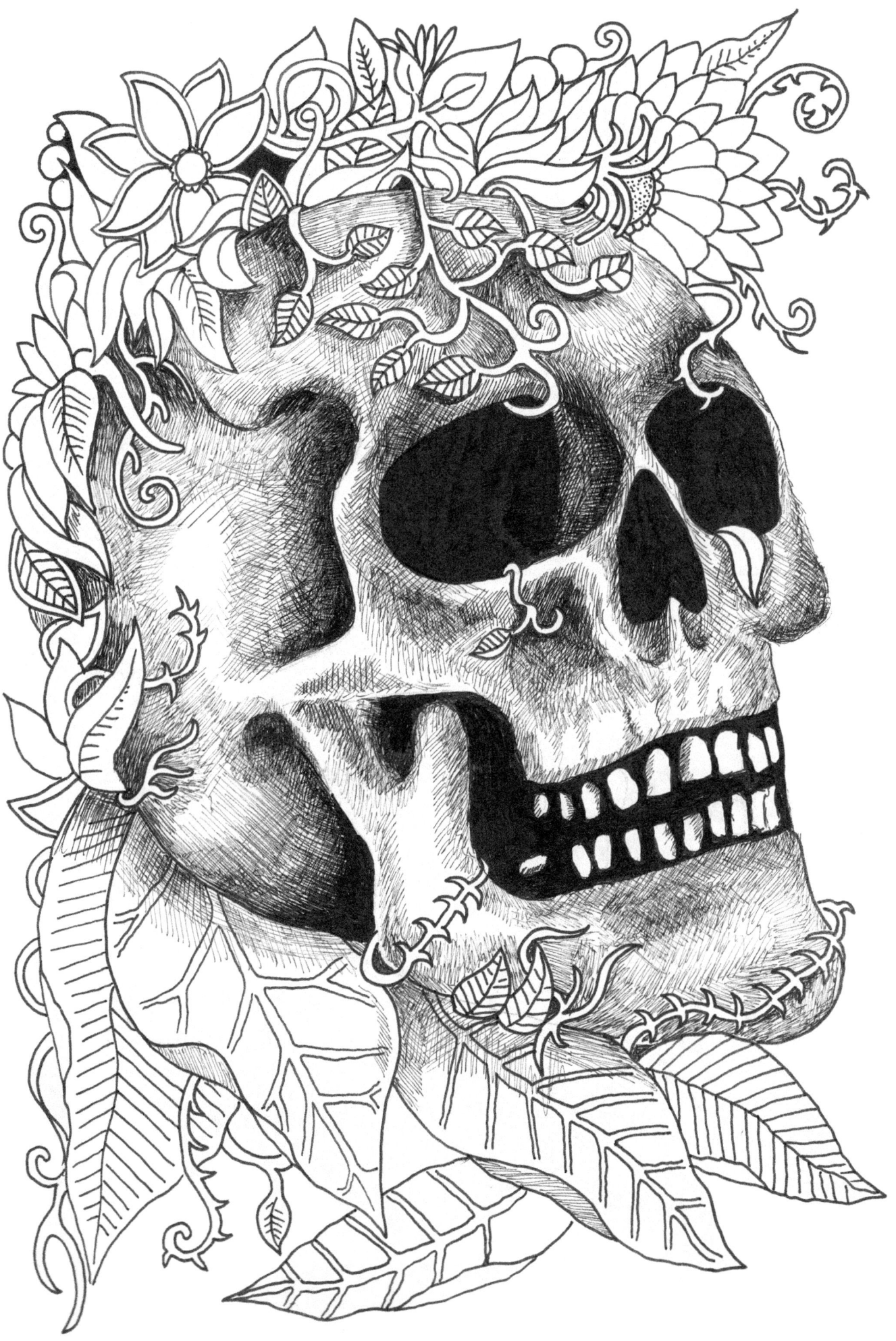

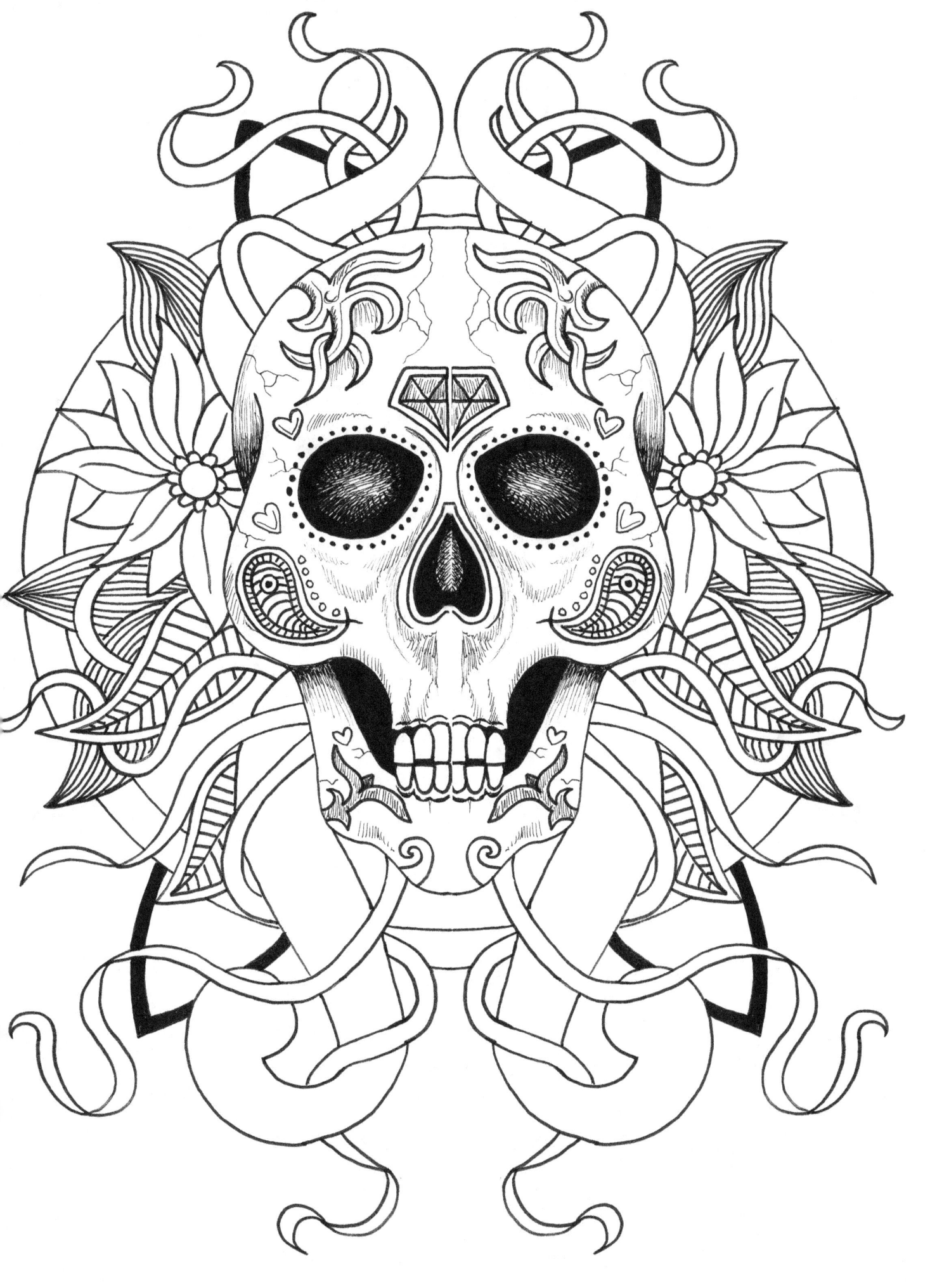

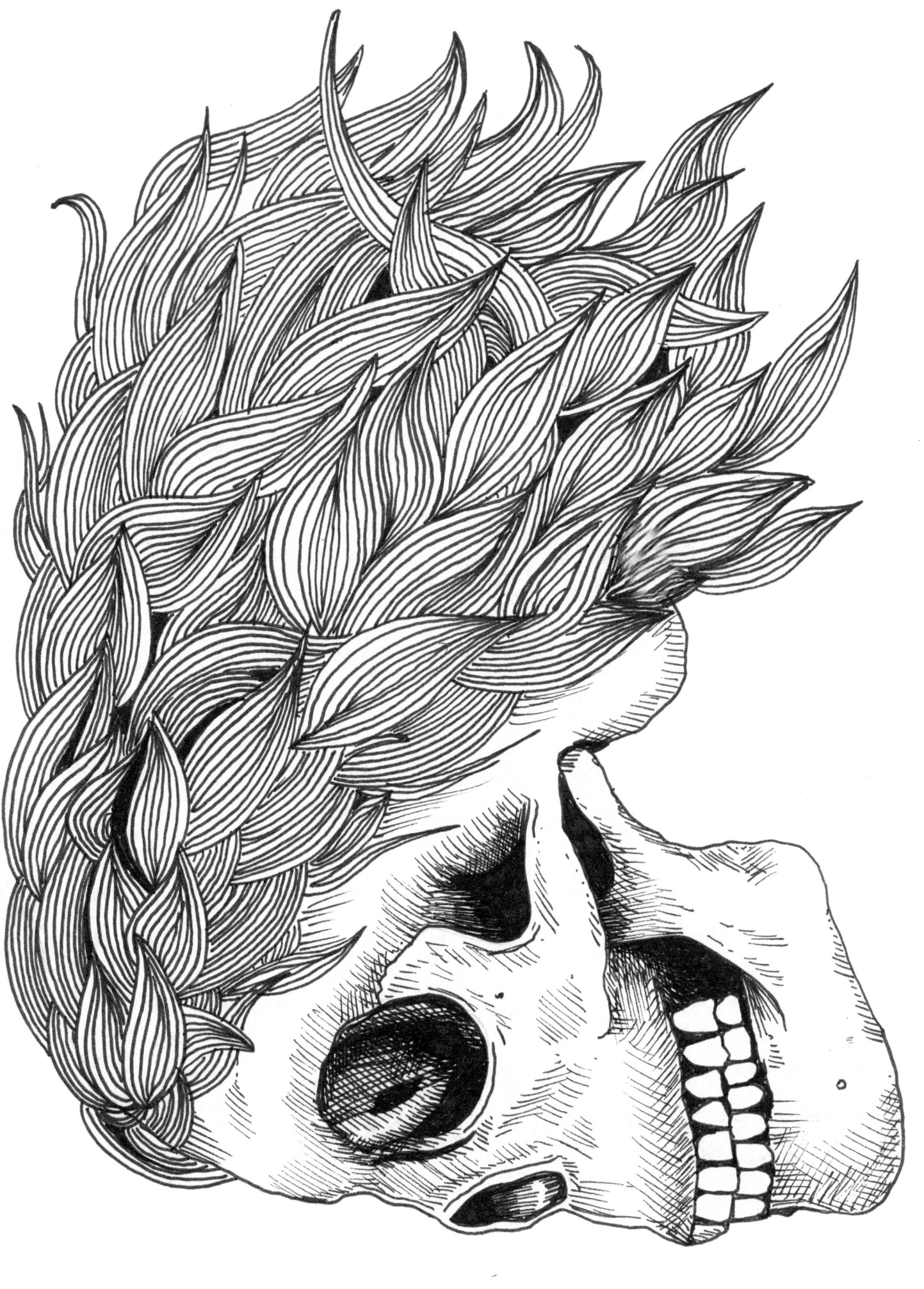

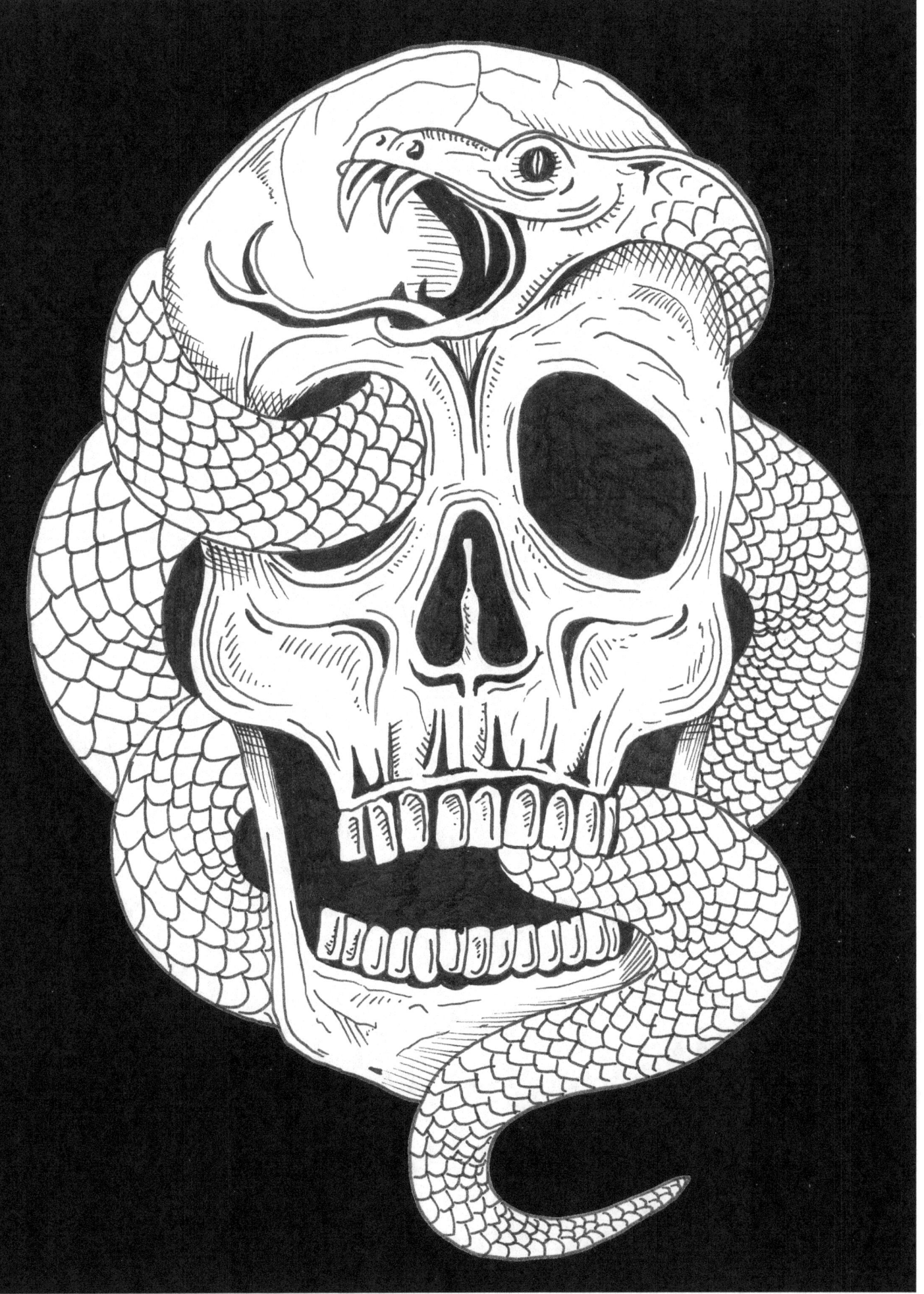

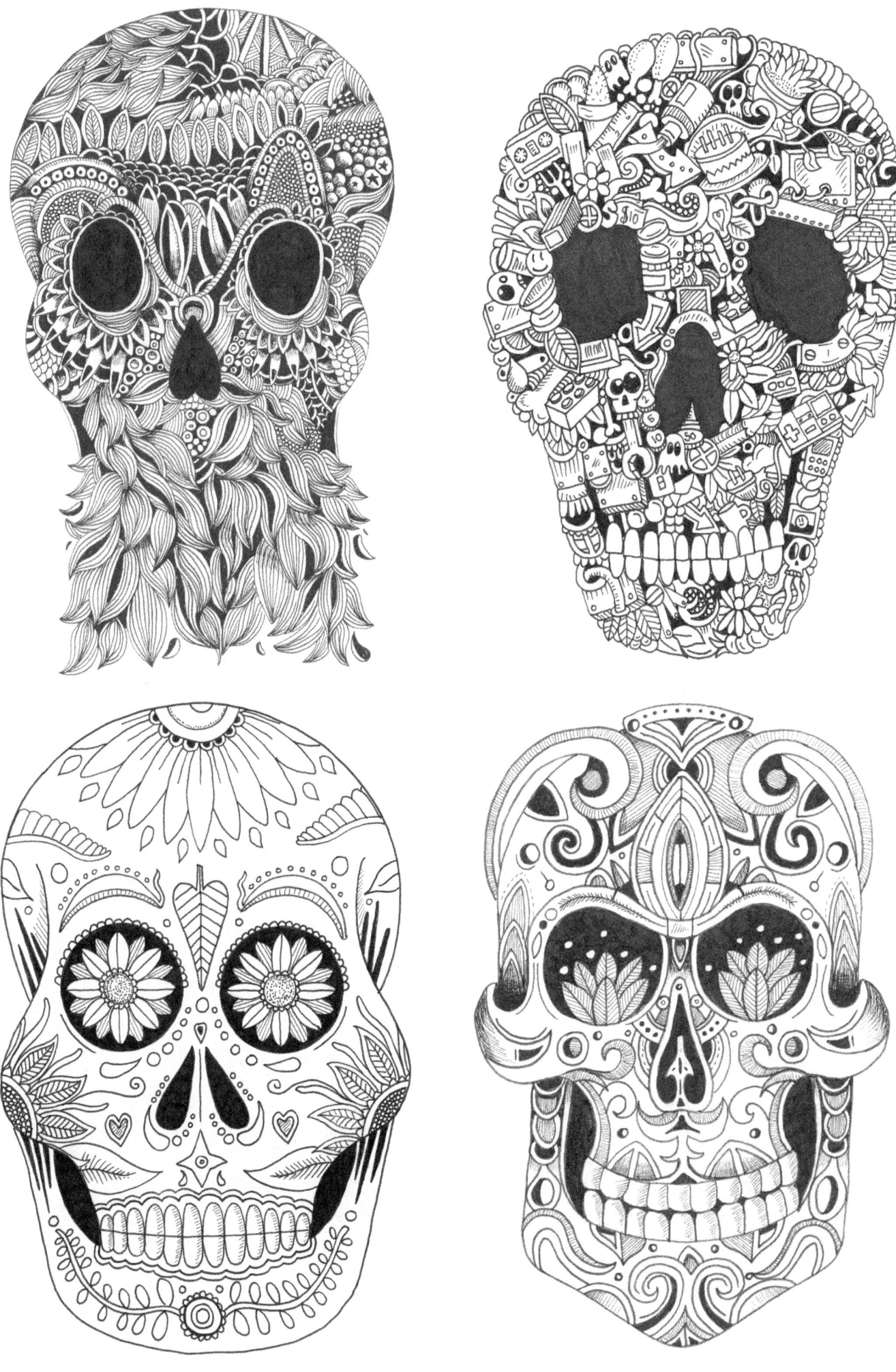

...other Squidoodle coloring books available

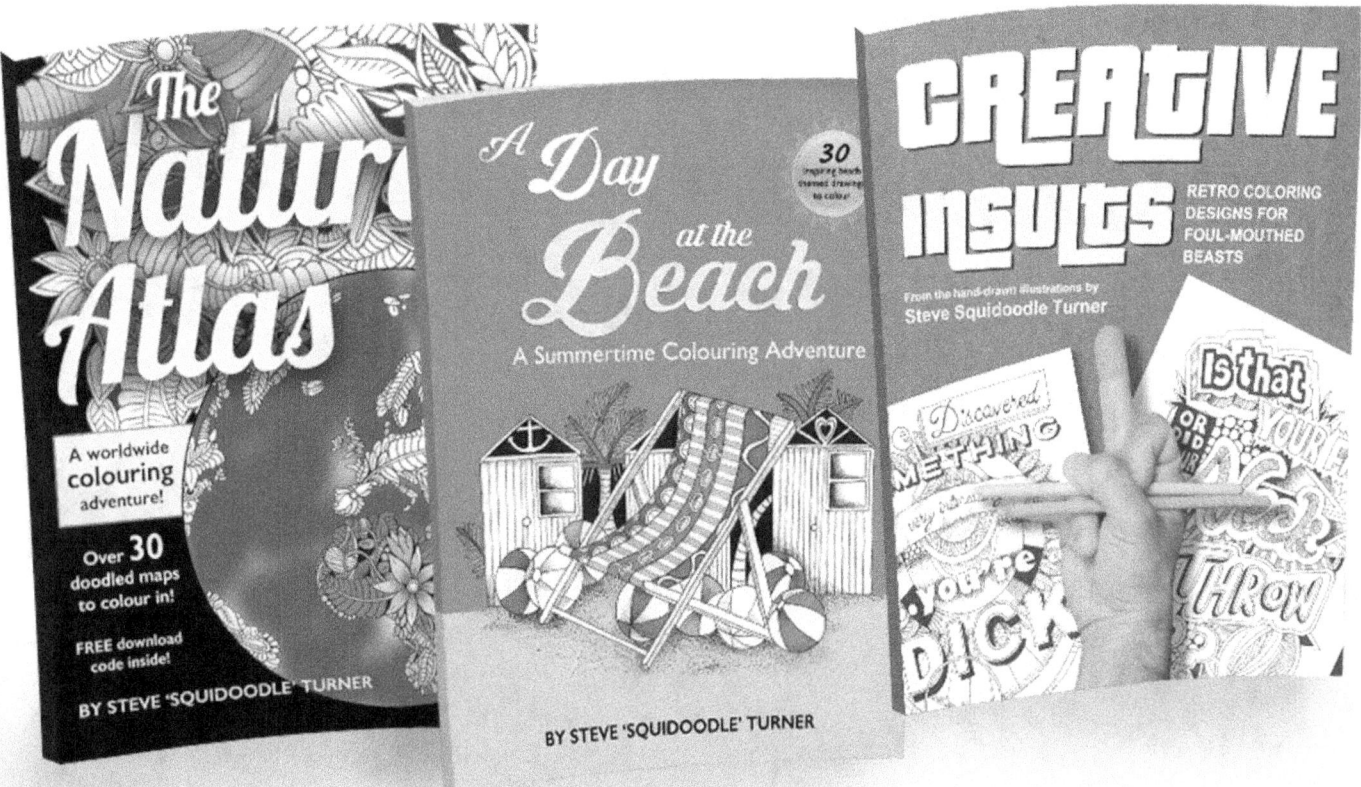

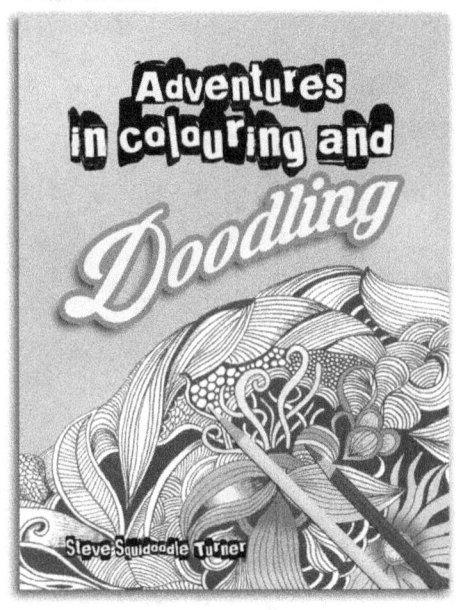

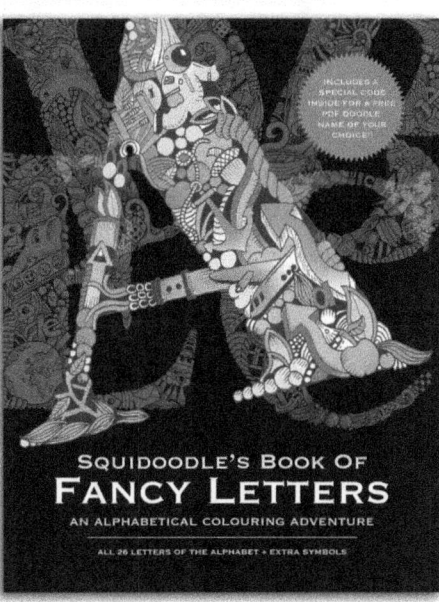

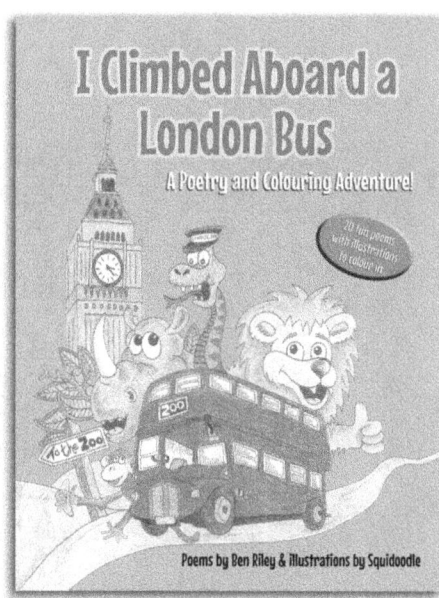

For original artwork, prints, greetings cards and **FREE** downloads, visit www.SquidoodleShop.com

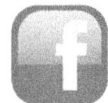 Get in touch! www.facebook.com/SquidDoodleArt

Test your colors on these mini-skulls...

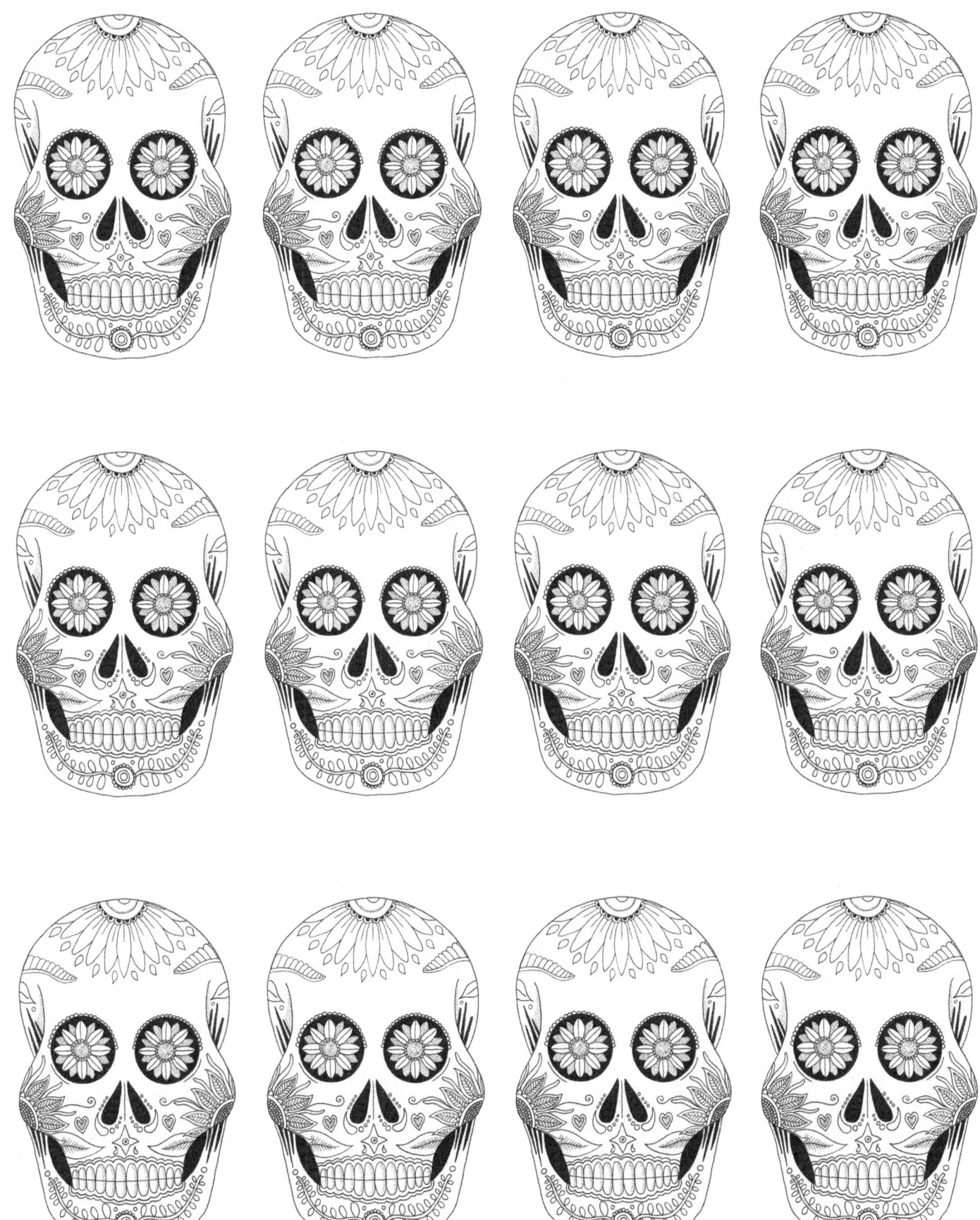

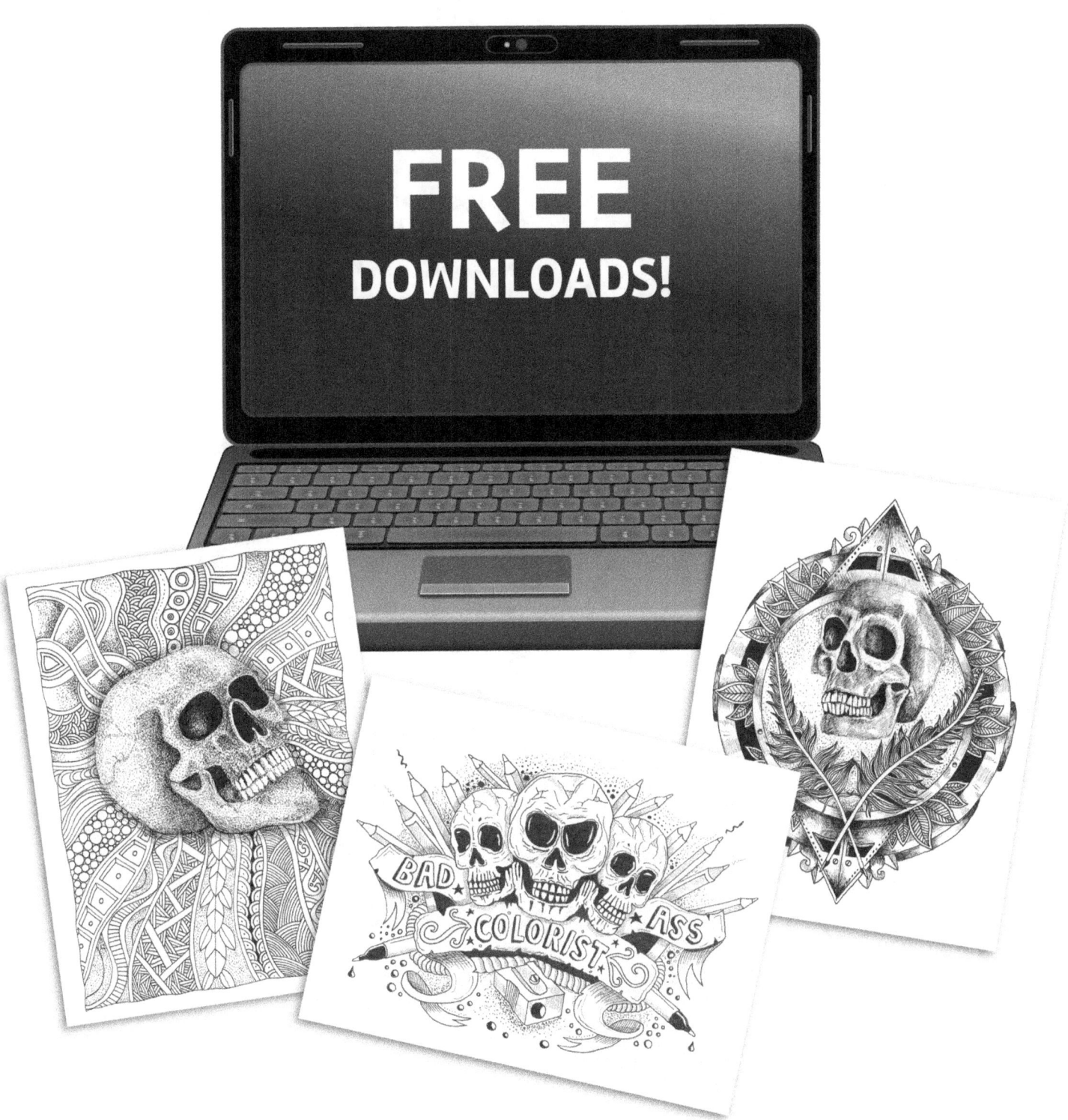

Freebie time!! You can download three pages from this book: Cranial Tapesty, Bad Ass Colorist and Skulls'n'Quills. Simply visit www.squidoodleshop.com, sign up for my email newsletters, then visit the "freebies" section of the website. Here you'll find these three pages alongside loads of other free downloads for coloring. Enjoy!!

www.ingramcontent.com/pod-product-compliance
Lightning Source LLC
Chambersburg PA
CBHW081851170526
45167CB00007B/2967